REVITALIZE Your Life
A Mind-Body-Spirit Makeover

REVITALIZE
Your Life

A Mind-Body-Spirit Makeover

Dr. Christine Rattenbury

REVITALIZE Your Life: A Mind–Body–Spirit Makeover

Copyright © 2010 by Dr. Christine Rattenbury

ISBN: 1453853103
ISBN-13: 9781453853108

Graphic Design by Holly Yvonne Designs, www.holly-yvonne.ca
Line Editing by Liz Taylor Rabishaw

Visit **Revitalize Your Life** @www.LivingMost.com

DEDICATION

For the other half of my heart, my husband Warren,

For the ones who encouraged my passion for all living things — my mother Lynn McKenna, my stepfather Bernie McKenna, and my late father Doug Rattenbury,

For my Rattenbury and McKenna families,

For fellow animal lovers and Mother Earth fans,

And for all those who wish to be uplifted and be a source of inspiration to others,

I dedicate this book to you. May the words of this book revitalize and uplift you, and may you fall in love with life all over again.

Chris

TABLE OF CONTENTS

INTRODUCTION

Welcome to the start of your mind–body–spirit makeover!

Sometimes we can't see the forest for the trees. Sometimes we can't see the trees for the forest. In truth, we need to see and embrace all of it, both the Big Picture of life and the Small Picture, the whole of it, in order to find happiness. Who-you-really-are is a tri-part being — mind, body and soul. All parts of you, the *whole* of you need to be functioning in harmonious, dynamic alignment in order for you to achieve maximum happiness and health. Here on Earth, the cutting edge of creation, the intelligent energy that is *you* is on a journey to experience the physicality of life, grow and expand. The Universe then expands through you. Perhaps you are thinking you ought to be enjoying the journey more. If so, it is time for a mind-body-spirit makeover! In order to fall in love with life (the forest), you must first fall in love with *all* aspects of yourself (the tree!)

The intent of $\mathcal{R}_{\text{EVITALIZE}}$ Your Life: A Mind-Body-Spirit Makeover is to offer you insights and new perspectives on the Big and Small Pictures of life. This fresh take on life will encourage you to shift your thinking and expand your awareness and in so doing, open you up energetically to flow more easily with life and have a better life experience. As you read it, try to step out of the confines of daily life and take in a broader, existential view of it all. A shift in awareness or consciousness produces a shift not only in your mind but in your body as well. Information is a form of *energy*. It has the power to *move* you. A shift in your thinking, one aspect of your tri-part self, will affect the other aspects of you. There are no true divisions between mind, body and soul. Where the mind goes, the body will follow! Your perspective on the meaning and purpose of your life strongly affects your mental and physical well-being and your overall satisfaction with life. Also, personal meaning helps you to cope with day-to-day stress and extreme stressors such as trauma, illness or chronic pain.

When people are preoccupied by their problems, their world view and mind set shifts in very unhappy and unhealthy ways which distorts or blocks their being's healthy energy flow. Life narrows or folds in upon itself. Fears grow. One is no longer able to go with the flow of life. Entropy replaces growth and expansion. Unhappiness, boredom or depression replaces contentment and fulfillment. Illness replaces health.

The path to a good life – meaning feeling happy and being well – is through *wholeness*. It requires that your mind, body and spirit are functioning in a concordant vibration of healthy energy. If you focus on well-being in only one aspect of yourself, without paying equal attention to the well-being of the other aspects of yourself, something will always elude you, be it health, self-worth, peace or a sense of fulfillment in life. *The way to happiness is through wholeness* and this book will help you achieve it. It will expand your awareness to encompass all of life and all aspects of who-you-really-are—mind, body and soul. It will expand your concepts of: what it means to be alive; how you view the rest of life all around you and your connection with it; how you view your journey through life; and how you view your physical body. It will help you to put your worries, physical problems, and daily ups and downs against a different backdrop, a larger frame of reference. Then, see what help a different perspective will bring. For maximum joy and health in living, wellness needs to be facilitated at every level, including your outlook on life. It is time to revisit the wonder and the true marvel of the life all around you and coursing through you. It is time to approach your well-being in a holistic and inspired way! It is time to revitalize your life and fall in love with life again!

My personal journey to find greater happiness led me to start exploring and expanding my own awareness of life. I have always had a passion for all living things, especially animals. My love of the natural world led to my pursuit of a science degree with a focus on biology. However, the human element was equally important to me, so I expanded my studies to include psychology and established a private practice in clinical and counseling psychology. However, as much as I valued the natural world and working with people and still do, I felt like something was missing—there was something more in the Grand Scheme of Things I wanted to understand and embrace in my life. My quest for fulfillment led me to the exploration of metaphysics and to study the written works of many inspired minds on the subject. In hindsight, I was embarking on my own mind, body, spirit makeover. I wanted to maximize my well-being and help my clients do the same. I now understand that in order for an individual to attain fulfillment in life they must seek well-being in all aspects of themselves, which includes not only their mind and body, but also embracing their higher consciousness i.e., the qualities of their spirit or soul.

REVITALIZE Your Life: A Mind-Body-Spirit Makeover explores what is meant by that and how to do just that.

There is an intelligent design for life—to expand and reach ever upward. Without expansion or growth, there is stagnation and death. Life meets its purpose—expansion—through a process called change. It is forever recreating itself, moving to the next level in its expression of itself. You are a beautiful and amazing manifestation of life, journeying to *your* next level—the next great and grand version in your expression of yourself. Are you ready to permit new perspectives and information to move you to your next level? An aspect of your tripart being must be ready or you wouldn't have bought this book! Life keeps drawing new opportunities to you for your growth and expansion until you embrace them, until you get the learning and move on. This book invites you to expand your awareness, shift, move, change, make a quantum leap to the next level of you—and feel happier and more in love with your life as a result.

As you grow, heal and elevate the energy that is you, not only does your energy shift in positive ways, so does the energy of the whole planet. The best way to restore the whole of planet Earth is for each individual to restore the part of the whole which is them. Our own being and the entire natural world needs each of us to do a mind-body-spirit makeover. Today, we are more aware than ever before of the power of the mind to create the physical reality we live in. We are also aware of our interconnectedness with all of life, its importance, sensitivity, sacredness and the impact that a shift in energy has on its, and consequently our own, well-being. We need science i.e., the wisdom of the mind *and* an inspired, intuitive approach i.e., the wisdom of the heart (or soul) to join forces in order to find the solution to our shared global problems. Today, with the combined forces of *science and the soul*, we have all we need, save the will to do it. The guiding principles of an advanced society are foremost unity (equality), love and benevolence. We need to consciously recreate the world in which we live so that it is not only a benign but an inspired place for all life forms to live and have *a good life.*

There are six chapters in this book, incorporating the "best of" wisdom of the minds and hearts of many to whom I am indebted. It is a synthesis of the inspired works of others passed through the filters of my own mind and heart, and my own life experiences as a junior biologist and a senior psychologist. Take your time with this information; pause often to contemplate it. I have endeavored to state what I believe are Cosmic Truths. It is not my intent to stir up controversy, or to try to convince you of anything. No one mind knows the "Right Answers". And, there is no "One Truth". You will pass this information through your own filters and decide for yourself what you think. It is my intent, however, to *stir you up* and to inspire you to expand your thinking and your heart and to reach for your own highest values and dreams.

REVITALIZE Your Life: A Mind-Body-Spirit Makeover is the realization of a desire, a reason d'etre that I didn't know I had until my own heart wisdom or spirit, with assistance from others, gave me a big nudge. It is the accumulation of much effort via help from brilliant written works before me, and my own determined efforts to lift myself and others up. It is my heartfelt desire this book will inspire and enable you to lift yourself up. And as you reach up and pull the higher, loving qualities of your soul down to help yourself, in so doing you will lift all of life up with you.

Chapter One

IN THE GRAND SCHEME OF THINGS

Take a few deep breaths and let go. Open your mind and let your thoughts expand. Here you are in a physical body having a life experience on planet Earth. Why are you here? What is it all about? You have been born on a planet with such an incredible, awe-inspiring, mind-boggling diversity of life all around you. Everything you can imagine is here. Every experience you can imagine happening, happens here. Every adjective that you can think of that could possibly describe an event, circumstance, or thing applies here in life on Earth — wonderful, amazing, awful, interesting, boring, ugly, beautiful…and the list goes on. The conscious, intelligent energy that is *you* — or who-you-really-are — chose to be here, in physical form, in this lifetime of yours on this planet. Why? And while we are contemplating the Grand Scheme of Things, just who are *you*, really?

Who are *you*, really?

The answer to this question depends on the perspective you take. Life takes on a different manifestation as you move from the so-called "more gross" forms of it (by that I mean the larger, or more substantial forms of life) to the "more refined", "subtler" or "higher phases" of it. For example, water is a "less gross" form of ice. Steam is a more refined or higher (less gross) phase of water. Higher phases have faster vibrations. We can view life from the perspective of "matter", "energy", or more refined or subtler still, we can view life as "intelligence" or "thought". A higher phase or more refined manifestation of thought can be distinguished as "consciousness". All manifestations of life are not really separate, rather one "blends" or "morphs" (for lack of better descriptors) into the other. One is a more refined version or a higher manifestation of the other. All manifestations of life are really different phases of *one manifestation.*

This one manifestation is the Source of all life, the Source of everything in the Universe, the Source of all matter, energy, intelligence/thought, and the Source of all consciousness. What *exactly* the Source *is* (a tiny "drop" of which is the *essence* of *you*) is unknown. How do we define such as Source? If there is one Source of it all, or an "absolute Source", then, as all means *all,* the Source would be the "All-That-Is": i.e., everywhere and everything—eternal, infinite, omnipresent (all or one matter), omnipotent (all or one energy), omniscient (all knowledge or one mind), and that which is the all or one consciousness. Wow!

This would mean that *you* are really matter, which is really energy, which in a higher phase and faster speed of vibration is really intelligent thought, which is in turn, an aspect of consciousness. Or, to put it in another way still, *you* are a *center-of-consciousness,* an aspect of the One Consciousness. *You* are in *essence* an extension of the absolute Source — a "relative" of the "absolute" — presently focused in this physical space-time reality. So is everyone and everything else. Your consciousness is now focused on experiencing physical life. *You* are consciousness (non-physical), an aspect of which is currently manifested in physical form. In the physical or relative world, your body is flowing with intelligent energy. A drop of which is from the great ocean of all life.

And while you are wrapping your mind around these ideas, allow me to pose another Big Question: *Why* does the Source separate itself into its relative parts, which go on a brief evolutionary journey, only to have them return to it once again? What is the sense of it all? What is it all about? Is it all about evolution and expansion? If the All-That-Is is *all*, can the *all* get, well, *"all-er"*?! Is there something *more* still? Does the Source have a Source? Will the energy field that is the Universe expand for eternity or will it ever cease to expand? For centuries, man has searched for the answers to such metaphysical questions about the Source and meaning of life and the nature of the Universe that surrounds him. Some believe they know all of the "right" answers, or at least some of them. Everyone has an opinion about what the Source of it all is and what to call it. Sooner or later, we have to call it something, be it: "Source", "Spirit", "God", "The Divine", "Universal Intelligence", "Highest or One Consciousness" and the list goes on. But the Source is *not nothing* for only nothing can come from nothing.

Man's first ideas about the underlying meaning and cause of life and the Universe were crude and fanciful, involving numerous gods, not to mention devils. With further thought on the subject, man's ideas have evolved and split among a variety of perspectives and teachings as presented by priests, yogis, philosophers, theologians, scientists, physicists, metaphysicians, etc. As time goes by, the different perspectives have begun to overlap and have arrived at many common understandings. More and more, debates are about finer points and semantics. When all search for the same Thing, they must eventually meet.

The true nature of the Source and meaning of life remain under the heading, "The Great Mysteries of Life". There are no definitive answers to these questions. There are no answers because *there is no "One Truth"*. A central finding from the study of quantum physics is that nothing that is observed is unaffected by the observer. In other words, science tells us that *all truth is subjective*. Because everyone is creating what they see, everyone sees a different truth. Put in another way, the place from which you are observing life determines what you see. *Perspective is everything*.

Ultimately, and hopefully, it is left up to each individual to find their own answers regarding the Source and the meaning of life. However, we cannot rely purely on the intellect for this, for attempts to contemplate the full meaning of the grand concepts of the Universe including infinity and eternity, or the absolute Source of all life, leaves the mind reeling and swimming. The great questions of metaphysics cannot be answered by the human mind. However, our sciences are firmly grounded in the laws of the mind. Consequently, science is left struggling to find the answers and must be satisfied by incomplete and sometimes contradictory explanations. We have a general idea of these grand concepts based on the definitions we assign them. But we are unable to grasp the full sense of the words—the mind of man at its current state of evolution or unfoldment cannot *truly and fully know* their meaning.

Fortunately, our intellect is not our only source of guidance. At times we may not know things, but we do have a *sense* of them. We can go by what *feels right*. One may *feel* that there is something more, something incredible, a purpose to it all, but one is left to take it on faith in the heart because the mind simply does not know. We are left to feel things when we do not understand them or when our mind does not know what to do about something. Your *true or natural* feelings arise from the wisdom *inherent in your body.* Your true feelings or *"heart's wisdom"* emanate from the aspect of you that is higher consciousness. They are a form of guidance for you from the wisdom of your higher or non-physical perspective while you navigate through physical life. The challenge is to hear and trust your true feelings or heart's wisdom. They can be quite subtle at times — a "gut feeing" or a quiet whisper in "the back of your mind". Your *body in the form of feelings* will try to tell you what your *mind may not yet fully know.*

We may never know the *What* and *Why* regarding the Source and meaning of life and the mysteries of the Universe but we know something about the *How.* As science advances we do obtain further knowledge.

Life as viewed from the quantum perspective

Whether you are looking at the Big Picture of life through a telescope or the Small Picture of life through a microscope, you will see the same thing: an organized system of spheres or particles of matter orbiting at great speeds through vast space around a center or nucleus. Peer deeply into the subatomic structure of a cell, of anything, even things that appear inert and are not typically categorized as living organisms, and you will see "a small Universe". The atom resembles a miniature solar system, with light, negatively charged subatomic particles (electrons) orbiting the dense, positively charged nucleus, just as the planets orbit the Sun.

Neither outer space nor inner space is chaotic. All matter, which is in motion, is organized and operating according to a precise design, clearly indicating that it is part of a larger and intelligent system. The macrocosm and the microcosm are virtual duplicates and they are both held together by some unseen yet obviously present and pervasive energy or force. Something drives outer space and inner space alike. It is an energy system that cannot be seen but its effects can be seen everywhere within and without. The same invisible, inconceivable, force drives both the solar system and the human cell.

All of space, inner or outer, is organized and operated by an incredible presence, a level of energetic intelligence beyond the mind's ability to fully and truly grasp. The space you see, the so-called void, appears empty and lifeless, but it is not. Nature abhors a vacuum. As stated, only nothing can come from nothing. Space may be dubbed "nothingness" because *no thing* is visible, but it is not dead. It is brimming with unseen, intelligent energy, literally teaming with energy in "virtual" form—energy that is *pure potential*, waiting to become material reality.

Our senses and sensibilities are not prepared to see the apparent nothingness or stillness that underlies everything in our world, everything in our Universe, as the birthplace of all of which we call reality. The exploration of outer or inner space takes us to the emerging world of quantum or particle physics. The study of quantum physics provides the beginnings of a bridge to aid in understanding and reconciling what we know about the material reality we can see and what we seek to know about life's true nature and origin. Instead of regarding the space between things as a lifeless void, if one could see it through the physicists' eyes, they would know that it is packed with intelligent energy waiting to emerge and coalesce into atom-life.

There is an energy field underlying everything outside and inside our world, including our bodies, which crystallizes for a brief period of time into intelligent, organic molecules. The experience this bit of life collects while it is in the material world will alter it. This bit of life will *evolve*. Hence the energy field to which it returns will change and evolve also. This ever-evolving energy field, which has no known bounds, is the starting point for everything that exists in the material world. Matter is a lower phase or a less refined manifestation of this energy. Everything we call matter comes from the subatomic energy field. This starting point of all that we call life is always in contact with every other point. There are no breaks in the continuity of the subatomic field. This rich field of silent intelligence functions as *one*. Hence the expression, *all of life is one*. Every bit of life is connected with every other bit of life. *There is no true separation*. There is one all encompassing energy at the core of all we see in material reality, or the relative world. There is one source for all the building blocks of everything we call life—and it is this invisible field of intelligent energy. All matter comes from this energy field and returns to it. The subatomic field is everywhere. It is the so-called void or space around all things. And it is ever expanding.

In true keeping with its paradoxical nature, life is ever so complicated while at the same time ever so simple. The vast diversity of life that you see all around you is in its essence, *the same*. All of life is made from the same basic building block. This is what is meant by the expression, *the universality of all matter*. What we call the building block and what we know about it depends upon the perspective from which you view or study it—whether you look at life from the "level" or perspective of matter, energy or intelligence. *Perspective is everything*.

In the early 1800's, man's search for the origins of life led him to conclude that the smallest denominator, the origin of all life was matter—specifically, the atom. Later, even smaller, subtler or more refined manifestations of life, the subatomic particles, were discovered. The term "particles" is used loosely as most of these so-called particles have almost no mass. Some have no mass at all. They are "blurs" of energy—energy in motion or vibration. With the discovery of subatomic particles, matter "gave way" to energy as the Source of the origin of life. However, at a more refined or faster vibratory level still is yet another manifestation of life, invisible but no less real, that being intelligence or thought. Thought, in turn, is a small aspect of consciousness which is hypothesized to reach levels of vibration so fast it is beyond our mind's ability to grasp. With further advances in our scientific understanding, energy has "given way" to thought or consciousness as the point of origin of life.

All manifestations of life are not really separate. One gradually blends or morphs into the other. Matter is a lower phase of energy. Energy is a lower phase of intelligence/thought. Thought in its highest phases and operations i.e., consciousness, is believed to approach the plane of the ultimate or absolute Source of all life. (Note: Thought is an aspect of consciousness. Thought cannot exist without consciousness, but consciousness does not need thought for it to exist.) The exact point intelligence/thought emerges from the Source (or One Consciousness) cannot be pinpointed or understood by the human mind. We are back to the realm of the Great Mysteries of Life and the Source of it all which is beyond the mind's present capacity to *truly and fully know.* In time, with the expansion of our intellect and consciousness, man may come closer to the full understanding that he seeks.

The Universe is full of magical things, patiently waiting for our wits to grow sharper.

Eden Phillpotts (1862-1960), author

Matter

Matter is the manifestation of life we are most familiar with because it is what we see all around us, and of course, matter is what the human body is made of. Atoms of matter "coalesce" or "crystallize" from the subatomic field for a brief evolutionary journey. Matter is a temporal focal point for energy. Before long, all atoms of life return to the source from which they came. Subsequently, they will spring from this energy field once again and move on to a new experience. This happens faster than you may think. Life is constantly on the move. Life in the form of the atoms in your body changes continuously. In fact, ninety-eight percent of the atoms in your body were not there a year ago! Atoms pass freely and continuously back and forth through the body's cell walls. The "container" of *you*, your body, is not frozen in time and space; nothing is. Everything you see, in its essence, is in motion and it is constantly changing. The solid, material world is an illusion. The senses fool the brain. It is only a perception that things appear solid or motionless. Subtler states of matter and energy underlie the observable outward appearance of solid matter. The nature of life depends upon the perspective from which you view it.

The forms that life takes will morph through endless incarnations. In this way, each atom of life will collect an ever-expanding array of experiences which results in its growth or evolution. Each atom will contribute a bit of this expanded intelligence to the new life form that it becomes a part of in its next metamorphosis, in its next cycle of evolution. Evolution is the way of all life, the way of the planet, the way of the Universe, the way of *you*. You are on the Earth plane to experience the physicality of life and while here, you will develop and unfold your potential. As a result of this Earthly experience, you will grow, expand and evolve. And, as you are a part of the Big Picture, the Big Picture will expand also. Evolution is not just the way of life on the Earth plane. It is the way of everything in the Universe.

Energy

After the concept of the atom was proposed by the early Greeks, further scientific advances led to the realization that atoms are in fact composed of smaller, subatomic particles of life, such as electrons. The electron was discovered in 1897. In 1911, it was established that the atom is actually a cloud of electrons i.e., energy in motion, surrounding a tiny, heavy core. Later, it was found that the core or nucleus of the atom is composed of protons and neutrons. By the early 1970s, it was discovered that these particles are in turn made up of several types of even more basic energy units, called quarks. Strong electromagnetic forces bind all the particles together. Bear in mind that a great deal of what we know about quantum particles is based on mathematical theory alone, because so much in the realm of quantum physics cannot actually be seen or studied directly. To date, more than a mind-boggling 200 subatomic particles have been identified. Most appear to have a corresponding antiparticle. Many physicists believe that the positive and negative charges of the Universe balance each other such that the net charge of the Universe is zero, or neutral.

From the subatomic perspective, everything is best understood as energy or light vibration. Matter in a higher vibration or finer form is the motion of energy. Higher phases of life's manifestations vibrate at greater speeds. When energy manifests into matter, it produces an illusion of solid, stable form. All that we know as material reality is an illusion, albeit a very persistent and convincing one! In truth, matter is in constant and perpetual motion or vibration. Paradoxically, motion allows us to perceive substance, yet our senses perceive matter as motionless. The mind is lost in the world created by the senses.

Stillness, or the point of zero vibration, is not a void but the starting point for everything that exists in the material world. Life in the form of waves of energy or light "pops" or "blinks" in and out of existence. It springs forth from the subatomic field and returns there. From this perspective of life, every thing, every thought, every emotion, every action is, in its fundamental form, energy in vibration.

Vibration is common to all things that we perceive as real or solid. It is the heartbeat of life. Each form of matter has its own rate of vibration or vibratory signature. Apparent differences in appearance of various life forms results from a different rate of vibration. *You* are pulsating to your own vibe — your body sounds its own note! And you thought you couldn't carry a tune! The primordial sound of Life is said to be, "Om."

All of nature is *alive*. And all of nature is in constant motion. The world of matter, or relativity, never rests. The relative world only appears at rest. All cell-life, molecular-life, atom-life is constantly changing and moving. This is the flow of life. Underlying all forms of matter is an energy pattern at a higher vibratory level constantly pulling matter into it and expelling matter from it. Atoms are continuously moving in and out of the apparent solid form. The shell of the form appears constant, but the atomic and subatomic life of the form is fluid and constantly changing.

Change is the way of all life. Chemical composition and decomposition are constant and everywhere. At the beginning of material life, there is a building up process. Life expands or evolves. Intelligent energy goes to work. Subatomic particles emerge from the energy field, the so-called void, and coalesce into atoms. Atoms coalesce until we have the appearance of solid forms. Lower (i.e., grosser or more dense) phases of life, have slower speeds of vibration. At the completion of the life form, there is a breaking down and a gradual "drawing in" process—more energy in motion, only this time, life moves in the direction of entropy not evolution. The dense solids of matter give way to liquids and then to the subtler or higher phases of gases and vapors and so on until life draws into itself—until it is again set into motion at the beginning of a new cycle. In your body, the planet, the stars, every where, work is constantly being done. Change is the only constant.

Intelligence and the conscious mind

Close study of energy affords a glimpse of the intelligence inherent within it. In some of its forms, it is possible to observe the intelligent action of energy as opposed to "blind" or "random" force. Life is characterized by organization and precision. Each manifestation that life takes, each step in the process of creation of the material world, is precise and orchestrated by intelligent design.

The whole history of science has been the gradual realization that events do not happen in an arbitrary manner, but that they reflect a certain underlying order, which may or may not be divinely inspired.

Stephen Hawking (1942-), physicist and author

That the Universe was formed by a fortuitous concourse of atoms, I will no more believe than the accidental jumbling of the alphabet would fall into a most ingenious treatise of philosophy.

Jonathan Swift (1667-1745), author and satirist of prose

Recent developments in quantum physics have resulted in revolutionary advances in scientific thought. In a higher or more refined phase, energy blends or morphs into intelligent thought or higher consciousness. With the discovery of even smaller particles of life, concepts and theories of energy have undergone radical change over the course of the past century. Subatomic particles are known to behave more like "mind-substance" than energy. From the perspective of quantum physics, science has arguably crossed the borderline separating mind and matter — more and more, mind and matter are seen as one. From this vantage point, the origin of life is best understood as mind or consciousness. Intelligence or mind underlies it all. All of life is, in its essence, a manifestation of intelligent thought, an aspect of *consciousness*. At this juncture, modern science dovetails with Old World and Eastern philosophers and sages who first proposed such an idea several centuries ago. Recall, when all search for the same thing they must eventually meet.

> *Quantum physics has been spectacularly successful in verifying what Eastern mystics have known for 2500 years. It is not our brain that gives rise to consciousness; instead it is our consciousness, or mind, that creates everything that seems so real to us.*

John Davidson (1944-), physicist and author

> *We are what we think. All that we are arises with our thoughts. With our thoughts, we make our world.*

Buddha (563-483 BC), philosopher, sage, mystic

Intelligence springs forth from the "void" and returns to it. It can manifest in less refined, increasingly dense forms. Matter in some form is necessary for energy to play upon. Intelligence must have matter and energy for certain expression. Mind uses its lower or less refined vehicles, energy and matter, as instruments, tools, or vehicles of expression. Today, science tells us that the expression *mind over matter* holds more literal truth than we ever thought was possible.

Then there is a further question of what is the relationship of thinking to reality. As careful attention shows, thought itself is in an actual process of movement... We haven't really paid much attention to thought as a process. We have engaged in thoughts, but we have only paid attention to the content, not the process...If I am right in saying that thought is the Ultimate Origin or Source, it follows that if we don't do anything about thought, we won't get anywhere.

David Bohm (1917-1992), physicist

As a man who has devoted his whole life to the most clear-headed science, to the study of matter, I can tell you as the result of my research about the atoms, this much: There is no matter as such! All matter originates and exists only by virtue of a force which brings the particles of an atom to vibration and holds this most minute solar system of the atom together...We must assume behind this force the existence of a conscious and intelligent Mind. This Mind is the matrix of all matter.

Max Planck (1858-1947), Nobel Prize for Physics, 1918

When the province of physical theory was extended to encompass microscopic phenomena through the creation of quantum mechanics, the concept of consciousness came to the fore again. It was not possible to formulate the laws of quantum mechanics in a fully consistent way without reference to the consciousness.

Eugene Wigner (1902-1955), physicist

The atoms or elementary particles themselves are not real; they form a world of potentialities or possibilities rather than one of things or facts.

Werner Heisenberg (1901-1976), Nobel Prize for Physics, 1932

I am now convinced that theoretical physics is actually philosophy.

Max Born (1882-1970), Nobel Prize for Physics, 1954

Energy follows thought (mind). Matter follows energy. This is the process of the manifestation of the material world. This is the process we all know as creation. All manifestations of life are variants of one manifestation. No separation exists. Matter is consciousness in a slower vibration. This would mean that the physical body is consciousness in a slower vibration. Everything in life, All-That-Is in the material or relative world, is an aspect of consciousness. Wow!

The conceptual boundary lines between mind, energy and matter are the result of man's sensory perceptions and limited capacity for understanding the vast complexity of life. Despite appearances, there are no true divisions. Division is an illusion. Just as division is an illusion between the mind, body and spirit. For all its strengths, the human mind cannot fully comprehend the vastness of life or the true nature of the forms life manifests in. We cannot fully grasp the extraordinariness of the ordinary. The mind of man separates and compartmentalizes the natural world in an effort to better understand it. We cannot possibly begin to understand it all without imposing boundary lines, categories, and our own rules upon it. With recent advances in scientific understanding, these man-made boundary lines start to blur and some fade away. However, perhaps no where are the artificial boundaries between mind and matter still so entrenched as in our understanding and approach to healing the human body.

Mind over matter

Particularly in the world of Western medicine, modern science is locked into a way of thinking which conceptualizes and treats a problem in a particular part of the body in isolation from the *whole of it*, and without adequate grasp of *what the body really is*—higher consciousness (mind), and energy (which coalesces into atoms and molecules of matter to form body tissues). Treatment protocols derived from the modern medical approach suffer from a predominant focus on matter and an inadequate focus on (or a downright denial of) the energetic or dynamic *mind-body connection*. Treatment focused exclusively on the problematic body part is missing out on the contribution from a *vital half of the equation i.e. the conscious mind* (or more accurately, the "higher" half of the equation, i.e. the higher vibrations of the mind).

The inner world is as impossible to *fully* grasp as the outer world. In response to a limited comprehension of the body's incredible operations as a whole (many believe we have just scratched the surface of it), man has had to compartmentalize and isolate bits and pieces of the whole story in an attempt to grasp it. This piecemeal approach to the scientific comprehension of the human body is understandable given the vast complexity of it. The intelligent energy which the body is comprised of is constantly on the move, both within it and through it. Nothing in the body is static, despite appearances. The biochemistry of your body literally and instantaneously changes with your every thought and mood. Your body is flowing with intelligence as surely as there is blood flowing through your veins. Any change in the body affects every other part of the body, instantaneously. The body truly resembles a river more than a solid, static form—flowing with ever changing, intelligent energy and atom-life. The flow of life does not stop to be analyzed. Nature defies the way our minds and science try to partition parts of it off from the whole, and apply our labels and rules upon it in a determined attempt to understand and explain it all. The inconvenient truth for medical science is that the body is never the same way twice.

The challenge of studying and treating such a fluid set of systems and structures is self-evident. Even though the physical body is a product of conscious thought (intelligence), energy and matter, modern medicine focuses predominantly on the "end product" or more gross forms of it i.e., matter (cellular tissue). The aspects of "conscious thought" and "energy" may be considered too abstract or vague and/or not amenable to the application of strict scientific method, so their importance has been downplayed or discounted. Often, we let our beliefs about what we "know" prevent us from seeing things *how they really are*. There are many such things in life that cannot be seen or readily studied while subject to rigorous controls in the laboratory. Subatomic particles are one example of that, love is another. For that matter, we have never been able to point to in terms of *matter*, exactly what tissues are responsible for some of the brain's principle functions: intelligence, memory, instinct and personality. How did the atom acquire intelligence, personality, love and compassion? It is not much of a leap to conclude that these functions or attributes are *not* based in *matter* at all. But rather, even though they are qualities the body has, they are not *of* the material body. They are manifestations locked permanently in *a higher phase than matter. They are not of physical form; they are of thought form.* They are the subtler, more refined qualities of conscious thought. And although they are not of matter, they are as real as the thoughts in your head, and influence the matter that you are. *The higher reaches of consciousness can heal the lower levels of consciousness (matter) because matter is consciousness in a slower vibration.* This is a crucial understanding and it is missing from modern medicine.

Any intent to devalue the importance of the contributions of modern medical science to physical health would be idiotic and that is certainly not my intention here. My point is this: notwithstanding the value of focusing on *cellular matter,* this is a *limited* approach to the challenge of creating healthy and lasting change in the body. Creation flows from the *top down*, from higher phases to lower, less refined phases i.e., from mind to matter. The *mind* is the "wild card" here: *our thoughts have a direct bearing on the creation and maintenance of healthy tissues in our bodies, or the creation and maintenance of ill health in our physical bodies.* Treatments developed from exclusive focus on the "end products" i.e., the unhealthy matter (tissues or body part), may lack efficacy and longevity, depending upon the nature of the physical problem as they have not evolved out of consideration of the powerful curative potential that the mind's thoughts can offer. Or, such treatments may fail to address the undermining and damaging impact of chronic unhappy and unhealthy thinking on the physical body. Drug therapy is an example of matter treating matter — chemical molecules treating the molecules of the body. While most would not deny the great value and effectiveness of drug therapy, problems arise when harmful side effects outweigh the benefits or when drug therapy is ineffective. What do we do then?

A focus on the mind-body connection is especially important when the nature of the physical problem cannot be clearly explained by the identification of a specific structural problem—rather it is a chronic problem of a vague or entirely unknown origin, such as the chronic back pain cycle, or many chronic diseases. In this case, there is no one identifiable body part causing the problem and no one drug that can cure it. These problems are systemic, meaning *whole*-body based i.e., *mind, energy and matter based.*

We need a quantum leap in our approach to healing the body which can only come about if we change how we view the body in the first place. Despite a lack of physical structure or tissue that we can point to, the body is a product of conscious thought (mind) and energy—invisible, but real. No doubt those pioneers who first bravely suggested the existence and importance of "invisible energy"—what we now know as atoms—were dismissed out of hand, or worse, at the time. History is full of such examples. Although we have just begun to explore the concepts and mechanism of action, recent research efforts which have broadened their scope and understanding of the human body to include a mind-body perspective have shown us that thought (including attitudes and emotions) and their resulting energy flow in the body play vital roles in the Big Picture of physical health and overall well-being. A focus on the mind-body connection is crucial for maximum health. Lasting good health and well-being can only be achieved with attention to the mind-body connection. *Mind, energy and matter, you are the whole of it and it takes a return to wholeness to fully heal.* (The mind-body connection is examined in greater detail in Chapter Four.)

Consciousness and levels higher

The existence and nature of the realms of higher consciousness is a contentious issue for some. Conventional science operates below a "glass ceiling". It does not allow for the higher manifestations of life that cannot be accounted for by solid evidence (matter). Consequently, science cannot explain the very real existence of the qualities of man's higher consciousness e.g., love, compassion, wisdom, intuition and creativity. Only *matter*, matters! Religion operates above the glass ceiling where only higher forces are important and adherence to them is demanded in the absence of real proof. The highest qualities of man are absent from the "lowly flesh of the body", reserved exclusively for the afterlife. *Matter* does not matter at all!

With science below the glass ceiling and religion above it, neither camp spans both realms. Neither perspective adequately incorporates and can account for all the phases of life's manifestations that exist in us and impact our daily lives. Both science and religion offer a narrow perspective on life — neither one is broad enough to incorporate the whole story. (Of course no one can fully solve the mysteries of the *whole* story; we are left to do our best with it.) Both science and religion do their share of reducing the marvel of the human body and the wonder that can be found in day-to-day existence to something rather cold and grim. With science, man's finest characteristics are denied or devalued as mere firings of neurons, or the actions of genes. Science turns a blind eye to the fact that genetics and neurons do not account for the basic functions of man such as his memories, personality, creative talents, aspirations, preferences, etc. With religion, man's life is under the control of unknown higher powers that he cannot prove, or readily access or have any say over (not to mention the problem of the highest, *most evolved* power displaying the *least evolved* characteristics of man, e.g., judgment, punishment and revenge).

Perhaps the apparent obstacle in both camps *is the answer* — that being the so-called glass ceiling itself. The glass ceiling that I am referring to is the *consciousness* that we are — which is also referred to as the *spirit* or *soul*. (Note: I use these terms synonymously: consciousness, spirit and soul. I also differentiate between spirituality and organized religion. I use the terms spirit and soul in the broader context of spirituality or metaphysics, devoid of any specific religious connotations. Pick the term and connotation you are most comfortable with.) Missing from science are the unique and higher qualities of man. Missing from religion is the real evidence of higher power and the idea that the higher manifestations of life are an integral part of man's everyday life which includes the body and the mind. *The soul is the missing link!*

The soul bridges the real world of matter and the equally real, higher and more powerful phases of life's manifestations. The existence of the soul or higher consciousness in every day life allows us to get past the barrier put up by science which is the insistence that material life is the only reality. The soul allows us to account for man's higher qualities, which are very real. And it gets us past the barrier created by religion which insists upon adherence to lofty forces with no basis in proof that we can point to in the real or material world. The soul gives us something real and tangible to look to in everyday life. Its here-and-now presence is apparent in so many ways, including our desires to learn and make improved choices and to pursue higher values such as wisdom, love, self-respect and respect for all life (not to mention that the physical body *is* a small aspect of the broader, higher consciousness or soul that you are, in a slower vibration). The wisdom of our soul or consciousness is active in our daily lives in the form of our *true feelings* which are the basis of our inner guidance.

Depending upon your beliefs, the concept of the soul can take on a broader spiritual or specific religious connotation, implying that it serves to connect life to a *Divine* Source of it all. Or, if you do not believe in a Divine Source, it can take on a strictly scientific meaning. Either way, it is your mind that forms your beliefs and chooses to participate in any spiritual, scientific or religious practices you may happen to believe in—your soul does not belong to any particular "camp"! The soul or higher consciousness is a Cosmic Force not a set of beliefs.

From the subatomic perspective, you are linked to the Source of all energy via the infinite quantum field—you are a "drop" from the great ocean of virtual life. The energy of this Source that you are a part of is so powerful and vibrating at such an unfathomable speed that it must be transformed at the juncture point of your physical body in order for you to survive. At the point of convergence with your body, this fast flow must be diminished or reduced to a trickle (much like the electrical energy of the main power grid must be reduced or transformed before entering the electrical system of your home). Your soul is the "dam" that stems the great flow to a drop in order for you to live as matter in the material world. Your body channels the energy and intelligence of the Universe, the same Source energy that creates planets and solar systems, *greatly moderated* by your soul. Your physical body is an aspect of your soul in a *slower speed of vibration*. Your soul is a Cosmic Force which conceives of and plays a role in all that you create while in physical form. It is an active part of you as you navigate through day-to-day life.

The soul is a subtler or more refined phase of the many manifestations of life that you are comprised of—matter, energy, mind/thought and higher levels of consciousness. All of these phases of life are operating in you, through you, *as you*. The soul is an aspect of consciousness. As such, it spans or permeates all the manifestations of life that *you* are—as water can permeate a handful of sand, oxygen can permeate water and subatomic life permeates the solid form. Your soul permeates the matter that you know as your body. The matter that is your body is a here-and-now aspect of your soul. Your soul is currently focused in the physical time-space reality of this planet *and* it occupies the realms of higher consciousness beyond the relative world and beyond our mind's ability to know.

Put in another way, your soul can be thought of as a bridge. It anchors you to material life at a slower vibration at the one end, and to the much faster vibrations of the higher planes, beyond the dimensions of time and space as we know them, at the other. *You* exist in the realms of the physical (bound by time and space i.e., the relative world) and the non-physical (unbound, eternal and infinite i.e., the realm of the absolute) *simultaneously.* Your soul makes it possible for you to be here in the material reality of the Earth plane i.e., in a physical body, while staying connected to the higher non-physical levels of you—on planes of higher consciousness reaching into territories unknown, to the Source of it all, whatever you believe that to be. Your soul is the broader perspective of you. It is who-you-really-are. You may also think of it as the unique aspect of Source that you are—your personality. (Although you are a unique aspect of Source, you are, at the same time, one with Source. A comparable analogy is that the fingers and toes are unique aspects of the body, but they are at the same time part of or one with the body.) You can always access the wisdom of consciousness i.e., your soul or the "older, wiser, broader you", through your inner guidance, or true feelings which resonate (vibrate) within your body (more on that in Chapter Two).

Your body is of the soul but it is not the entirety of your soul which spans levels higher than the physicality of the Earth plane. However, because the effects and operations of the soul in everyday life can be observed, we are able to form a meaningful concept of the soul and develop a real understanding of it, albeit an incomplete understanding of it. This is what we are left to do in the case of other realities, such as life in the quantum world, in the absence of physical, visible proof. Nevertheless, we cannot know *all* aspects of the soul while we are in our physical bodies on the Earth plane. The current level of man's conscious mind simply cannot expand enough to truly grasp the great heights of it all. We can define consciousness but we cannot *fully know* the extent of the consciousness that we are. We are aware of being conscious in everyday life, but at the same time, our consciousness extends to higher levels beyond the mind's present ability to be fully aware of, to fully know. The mind of man is bound by its current state of the evolution of his consciousness while living in physical form on this planet. In time, as our conscious awareness evolves in this time-space relative world, man's conscious awareness in physical life may broaden to encompass greater heights, higher planes of consciousness.

What are the higher planes of consciousness beyond the level of everyday life that our soul links us to? Many people believe in and claim to have experienced higher planes: for example, the psychic plane, where one can access their extrasensory perceptions or the so-called sixth sense, or the astral plane (believed by many to be the spiritual plane or plane of consciousness beyond the physical plane) to name another. For centuries, man has reported experiencing moments of expanded consciousness which allowed access to such higher planes. Once again, we are back to the questions pertaining to the Great Mysteries of Life and the vast unknown — of which man is permitted occasional glimpses.

To become aware of the consciousness that is *you* in everyday life, try this simple exercise: try to picture yourself dead. You cannot do it because who-you-really-are cannot die. While you are looking at your dead body in your imagination, there is still a part of you alive and well doing the *observing*. In this moment, you are aware that there is more to you than your body. There is something "in the back of it all" and that something is your consciousness or soul — that something is actually someone, *you*! Think of the common expressions we all find ourselves using from time to time, "I see myself doing that." And, "I know I need to change what I am doing." Who is "I" and who is "myself"? You are not two people, but you do exist in two different realms — the Earth plane (realm of the relative) and the soul plane (realm of the absolute). The silent observer of the self is always present. It is the "I" that sees your "self". It is your so-called "higher self" or soul. Your soul or spirit is the broader perspective of you which knows no bounds. And if you are alert to it, if you make a point of being conscious of it, the important guidance or wisdom your soul has for you will make itself known to you in this physical life of yours. Guidance from the soul is subtle. It comes as a whisper of a voice or a quiet dawning of *awareness* – unlike the voice of the mind which is frequently screaming at you. You may not "hear" your soul's wisdom, even though it is sometimes described as "the little voice in the back of the mind", you will *feel* it or *just know* it.

This is everyday evidence of the consciousness that *you* are, of the very real existence of your spirit or soul in the here and now, not just at some loftier height. It is the part of you that is *aware* of yourself existing, the part of you that is aware of yourself as a separate entity…an "I". The mind and body are always changing, as they are the "tools of the soul" i.e., the means by which your soul expresses itself, expands itself and evolves. They will eventually die and return to the Source of it all. However, your soul is everlasting. Your soul transcends the time-space reality of the relative world, the world of matter. The center-of-consciousness that you are is simultaneously rooted in present or relative time and absolute time i.e., the "forever" of all the tomorrows that you can imagine, and beyond.

The Great Debate

Unlike the mind, as the soul does not belong to any one camp, the soul can accommodate *both* the perspectives of science and religion at the same time, even if the mind of man cannot. Science, which is an undertaking of the mind, can only go so far in showing us what the spiritual quality of life is all about. A great number of people, whether or not they subscribe to any particular organized faith, feel that there is something more "behind it all" or something more within. Many *feel* that life and the quality of *being* is more than the sum of its parts, even if they cannot explain it. How do we harmonize the spirit (or heart) *and* the mind? The mind has great difficulty accommodating a point of view from two different perspectives at the same time. On the planet of duality, in a debate, the mind picks one side or the other as being right e.g., science *or* the soul, the head *or* the heart.

Some of the most debated metaphysical questions of all time are: What is the nature and meaning of life? What is the Source of it all? Is life the result of evolutionary processes which are Divine (i.e., planned) or is it the result of processes which are entirely random? These questions and more have been debated since the mind of man could first formulate them. Why? Because the *mind wants to know everything.* The mind is a source of evolutionary drive within us (as is the soul) — and as such, it keeps pushing us to expand. The mind wants to know what, why, how, when, who, etc. Acquiring knowledge is how it expands itself. But with many things on Earth, because of duality (polarity), there is an up side to them *and* a down side to them, and the ways of the mind are no exception. The mind thinks there is "One Truth" to everything — in fact it insists there is, it *knows* there is. It closes off to the possibility of more than one truth — the mind says that is not possible, not rational. More to the point, the mind is not *comfortable* with the possibility of more than one truth. The mind says such things as: either the head *or* the heart is right, pick science *or* the soul, life is either planned *or* random, something is right *or* wrong, inferior *or* superior, it's me *or* you. The concept of *both* creates anxiety in the mind when it is given the choice between two apparently disparate alternatives or poles.

The mind fears the possibility of more than one truth as it needs to be certain it knows what is real (of course, it defines reality as it knows it). It needs to know what is real and what to expect in order to think it is safe and secure. The mind decides for itself what is possible in life or not. The mind does not like the idea that a *change in perspective can change the truth of what is observed.* It is very threatened by this notion. The mind is a product of duality and thinks in terms of either "this" or "that". Things are either up or down, hot or cold, tall or short. For the mind, things *cannot be both.* The mind narrows its focus or its realm of possibilities, picks one side of an issue, problem or debate and eliminates the other side. This helps the mind to think it is secure in knowing what is what (the up or positive side of this practice of the mind). However, the mind can narrow its focus a great deal and shut out a host of possibilities life may present which keeps life feeling interesting, stimulating and worth living (the down or negative side).

As we age, this tendency to narrow and see and experience only a small part of the Big Picture, or only one side of an equation, tends to increase. This is fine if you happen to be happy and fulfilled with what is falling within the mind's narrow scope or focus in day-to-day life. But for many, this is not the case. Their minds have narrowed too much in pursuit of a sense of security. It is as though they are almost more afraid to live than to die. Unless you (from your broader perspective i.e., the "observer of yourself") keep an eye on the mind (the narrow or fear-based aspect of thinking), the mind can start to run the whole show of your life—and you may or may not like the results.

For the mind, the tendency is…there is only one truth and what is true cannot change with a change in perspective. However, *life* has other ideas…

There is no "One Truth"

The fact remains that life itself, the natural world, refuses to fully cooperate with the mind's comfort zone of duality, of either this or that—it sometimes chooses…*both*! Nature does not care about the categories the relative mind of man tries to assign to it. Nature defies mind. What would happen if we look at the nature, meaning and origin of life from a *broader* perspective? Could that which we declare as true, really and truly depend upon the *perspective* from which we view it? What happens to our view of life and its meaning if we *keep the mind open* to other possibilities? How might we *feel* about the life that is us, the life that we are living and the life that is all around us then? Is it possible that an open mind, a broader more *inclusive* perspective, may help us feel happier about ourselves and our life? Might opening our mind to the Grand Scheme of Things and the infinite possibilities of the wonder of life help us to enjoy the journey more? Let's see what a different perspective can bring.

The mind believes that science supports the idea of the one truth. We study things objectively, observe and measure the so-called one truth. But eventually and fairly frequently, science itself shows us the mind was wrong about that particular one truth. As we learn more, it is not unusual to learn that what we thought was right is indeed wrong. Then the mind has to adjust and admit to new things. You mean the Earth is not really flat? And the Sun does not revolve around the Earth after all? "Oh!" Mind declares. "That's interesting! I did not know that." In that moment, the mind opens to new possibilities.

However, the mind quickly goes back to its old ways of thinking, as the mind so often does. In this case, the mind goes back to its comfortable notion that we can indeed learn the one truth. We just adopt a new version of it. The mind is a "creation out of habit", a product of prior conditioning. The mind is based on past data, although it can update its "files". The problems we have in life are often the result of the mind (which is busy feeling inferior or superior or having other fear-based, egoic thoughts). And yet, the mind is what we have to work with. We cannot work very well without it!

Leading edge physics now tells us that *everything we observe is affected by the observer*. Wow! In the world of the small and the fast, different particles appear differently at different moments in time as observed by different people!

There is no such thing as passive observation. The experiencer is dynamically linked to the experience.

John Wheeler (1911-2008), physicist

Observations not only disturb what is to be measured, they produce it.

Pascual Jordan (1902-1980), physicist

In other words, a change in perspective does indeed change what is being observed. Wow! Oh! That is really interesting! Can you open your mind to this? *Each one of us sees and knows a different truth.* We do not all look at life through the same set of eyes. No two people see things in exactly the same way. This idea is not new, although the mind insists it has never heard it before. But now physics gives us the proof of this "Cosmic Truth". We do not tend to think this way because of the mind's conditioning, and most of us are not navigating through life peering through the world's most powerful electron microscopes. Plus, we only know our own perspective. Nevertheless, *science itself* tells us there is no one truth!

Could life as we know it be but an illusion? Could my eyes and ears really see and hear something different than yours do? Could all of life be but an impermanent shadow of the Cosmic Truth? Could life be but a dream and we need just row our boats merrily, merrily, merrily down the stream? The mind counters with—but if I cut myself, I bleed—are you saying that isn't real? Of course it is. But as always, what is seen as real depends upon the perspective from which you view it. We are so sure of the reality we live in. We think the platform on which life is built is so solid, so stable and so permanent. But in truth we are slaves to our five senses. We are using our physical senses to decipher vibration. What we think is so static and so real is changing constantly. What you see with your eyes is only a vibrational *interpretation.* What you hear, smell and feel are all vibrational interpretations. Buddhist philosophy says that truth is power and the ultimate challenge for every human being is to become strong enough as a soul to consciously realize Cosmic Truth while living as a physical being in the land of illusion.

> *The truth knocks on the door and you say, "Go away, I'm looking for the truth," and so it goes away.*

> *Robert Pirsig (1928-), philosopher*

How much Cosmic Truth can you absorb on this journey of illusion while still living within the illusion? You must decide for yourself what you believe your truth to be. Nature does not have a problem with this; it is the mind that has the problem. Life just keeps moving us along the path of expansion of our souls. The mind does not know what to do with this idea of illusion—it seems so irrational, so impossible. But there it is, nonetheless. The world is not flat. The impossible is possible. And there is no one truth. So what can we do when the mind feels threatened by the information facing it? ...*Open it!*

The only real voyage of discovery consists not in seeking new landscapes but in having new eyes.

Marcel Proust (1871-1922), author

Open the mind

This is the *amazing wonder* of the mind—we can allow it to stay closed to new ideas or we can choose to open it! Just as we would expect on the planet of duality, the mind can be closed *or* open. But can a part of us be closed and another part of us be open *at the same time*? Is that possible? Where does *your* mind stand on that question? *In this age of reason and intellectualism, we tend to forget about something below the neck—the heart.* What could be so much more powerful than the almighty brain? *The wisdom of the heart!* The heart has the power to *open the mind.* A vast amount of assistance in the journey of life can be gained from listening to the wisdom of the heart. It has the power to open the mind so that we can choose to think differently and feel differently about life. The heart allows us to *allow for* the other half of any equation—even if we do not like it or agree with it!

The heart is *inclusive* whereas the mind is *exclusionary.* The heart allows us to open our mind to consider to *both* sides of an issue or debate—the Big Picture. The wisdom of the heart leads us to have a broader experience of life. And the more we broaden to the *whole* of it, the more we flow with all of life instead of resisting it. The less resistance we put up, the better the energy of life can freely flow through the mind, body and spirit that we are. We are then more likely to feel happy about the life we are living. When we cannot *think* our way through something — when we just do not know what to think or what to do — we can come back to the *heart* and *feel* our way through it. Ask yourself, what do you know, *intuitively*? What is your "gut feel" about it? *The gateway to the soul's wisdom is first through the heart, then the mind.*

How we experience life is all about the perspective we take on it. One of the goals of this book is to offer you new perspectives so that you can shift your thinking if you choose to. The heart operates from a broader perspective than the mind. A shift to a broader perspective brings a broader life experience. It opens you up so that you can flow more easily with all of life. Broader is better — at least from the perspective of your soul or spirit — because you are here to grow and expand. And what is best for your soul is ultimately best for you!

We are all quick to narrow in on one side or the other of an issue. Everyone formulates opinions and tends towards exclusionary thinking (polarity or duality) because we are all living a physical life on a planet of duality, in a body which has a mind, and the mind wants one answer to a given question and believes there is only one answer. And while escape may be futile, it is possible to *transcend duality* for a moment and see life from the Big Picture perspective i.e., from both ends of the continuum, the whole of it. A shift in perspective can be transformative. Let us look more closely at the questions of the nature and origin of life to see what shifts a broader perspective in conscious awareness may bring.

What is the nature and origin of life?

Perhaps the debate about the nature and origin of life is more a debate between what a person thinks to be true (i.e., what your mind tells you, based on what you have been taught to believe) versus what they feel about and how they experience the natural world around them (i.e., what they intuit in their heart). Let us see how a dialogue or debate about the nature and origin of life might go between our two candidates in this debate, "Mind" and "(Mother) Nature".

Characteristics or descriptors applying to the candidate Mind are: One Truth (i.e., perspective is irrelevant), relative (i.e., duality or polarity), rigid, exclusive, brain's wisdom, scientific, logic, reason, objective.

Characteristics or descriptors applying to the candidate Nature are: Cosmic Truth (i.e., perspective is everything), absolute, flexible, inclusive, heart's wisdom, absence of proof, intuitive, faith, subjective.

Many individuals upon surveying these two opposing lists of characteristics have already picked the one set they are most comfortable with. Some might say they don't know which set they agree with. Few will say they espouse to both sets of descriptors because they appear to be mutually exclusive. In describing the following debate or dialogue between Mind and Nature about the nature of life, my intent is not to try to convince you to pick one side over the other. In fact, I am asking you to try *not* to pick any side at all. Try to keep the door of your mind open. Keep it open even if that means exposing it to a little discomfort. On the planet of duality, a little discomfort is good for you! Discomfort prompts or pushes you to make change and change leads to growth. It does not matter what answers you come to regarding the nature and origin of life. No one mind knows the right answers. Why not try on a few new perspectives and see if they fit you? A new perspective brings a new *awareness* to the questions—and awareness is *powerful*. Awareness has the power to shift your entire being. How your mind ultimately answers these questions is up to you. Look at what is possible regarding the nature and origin of life from the perspective of *both* Mind and Nature. How might a new awareness affect you?

At the outset of the debate, Mind has a problem arising from the approach it takes to life, which is from the perspective of the *relative* as opposed to the perspective of the *absolute*. Although we describe the Universe in absolute terms i.e., the continuums of time and space are known to be "eternal" and "infinite" respectively, we are unable to *experience* Universal life in absolute terms and so we put the absolute perspective out of our minds. We experience life in *relative* terms. And in viewing life from the perspective of the relative world, Mind imposes categories and polarizations on the wonders of Nature and the Universe. As stated, in the relative world, the world of duality, Mind says things must be either this or that, one or the other — they cannot be both. Mind is exclusive. It picks one end or the other of any given continuum describing life. In the relative world, life cannot be both short and tall, nor both fat and thin. And in the relative world, life cannot be both finite and eternal, nor both limited and infinite. Mind applies and embraces polarizations, categorizations and limits regarding the nature of life in an attempt to comprehend the great vastness and complexity of all of Nature, which leaves Mind reeling and swimming. Mind demands to know the one truth of life's nature and origin. Mind demands to know which side or which end of each continuum describing life is the right one. This quest for truth keeps man striving, learning, growing and evolving — until Mind is pushed out of its comfort zone and sensibility. Then Mind closes to new possibilities. Mind is prone to fears and readily becomes uncomfortable or threatened. When threatened, Mind can become judgmental, intolerant or think it superior. When Mind thinks its way is the right way and the only way, it locks down. Then Mind brings man's process of new learning and expansion to a screaming halt. When Mind narrows, life closes in on itself. This position is opposite to growth; it is closer to the end of life's continuum which is entropy or death, not evolution.

Nature accommodates all perspectives of life—both ends of any continuum. Life, including its origin, is not an either/or problem for Nature. Nature does not bother with categories or divisionary thinking. Nature rolls with it *all*. Nature *flows*. It flows where and how it wants. Nature operates with definite purpose and intelligence. (Mind cannot claim to always do that!) Mind excludes. Nature includes. Nature accommodates all perspectives, all manifestations of life, the *whole* of it—those that Mind knows about and those it does not, the finite and the infinite, the possible and the impossible, the magical and the mystical. Nature gives us bumble bees that can do what Mind says is aerodynamically impossible for them to do—fly; reef fish which can change gender from male to female; salmon which find their way back to their spawning grounds; whales that can do the seemingly impossible and navigate the global waterways to find their breeding and feeding grounds. In a flash, Nature creates a new planet and swallows up a star through a black hole. Although it takes part in the relative world, *Nature transcends the relative world at the same time*. When faced with the "either/or" choices of the relative world, Nature refuses to choose one or the other and instead chooses *both*. Fish can swim *and* fly. Birds can fly *and* run. Mammals can live on land *and* water. Snails can be both male *and* female *at the same time*! "Why not?" Nature says. "No problem!" it exclaims.

Nature does not cooperate with Mind's attempts to understand all of it or box it in with its rules. Nature defies Mind's relative world constructs. Just when Mind thinks it has Nature fitting nicely into its categories of this way or that way, Nature finds its own way. Nature manifests an inconvenient exception to the rule—an inconvenient truth! It is an escape artist. Nature favors exceptions to the rule as exceptions make the best survivors.

Life on planet Earth is full of paradoxes. Nature loves them. Mind does not. Mind's theories do not explain *everything*. But the Mind *wants* to explain everything. Once Mind settles on its position, chooses its camp and gets comfortable with its paradigm, Mind turns a blind eye to things that do not fit its sensibility. Its ears close; its door slams shut. It hunkers down for the debate. It clings to its certainty that it knows the one truth about the nature and origin of life. It knows the right answers. Nature counters with Cosmic Truth— the place from which one is observing life determines what one sees. *Perspective is everything*. Mind has been dealt a blow, but does not give up.

Nature at the particle level delivers all manner of remarkable, inexplicable findings. One such finding is that many atoms can co-exist in exactly the same place, at precisely the same instant in time without bumping into one another!?! Subatomic particles, which all of material life including our bodies are composed of, are sometimes particles, sometimes waves, sometimes seem to have a particular energy and sometimes not. Particles appear differently to different people at different points in time. It was necessary for a physicist (W. Heisenberg) to invent the Principle of Uncertainty (which has been described as, "Something unknown is doing we don't know what"!) as a fundamental Law of Nature in order to explain the problematic reality that both the precise position of a particle and its momentum cannot be known at the same time. Nature also gives us the phenomenon of twinned-photons. Two photons of light from the same source many miles apart will respond simultaneously to a stimulus applied to just one of them. These mysterious long-range connections that exist between quantum events, connections created from nothing detectable whatsoever, in theory can reach instantaneously from one end of the Universe to the other.

The quantum is that embarrassing little piece of thread that always hangs from the sweater of time-space. Pull it and the whole thing unravels.

Fred Alan Wolfe (1934-), physicist

What do these findings say about our concepts of space, of time, of life itself?! Is this level of intelligence and organization indicative of a plan of such monumental scope that we can not begin to fathom it?

Mind presses on…One aspect of the debate regarding the origin of life pertains to the concept of time. Mind says that evolution occurs in a slow, observable, linear fashion over the millennia. Evolution cannot happen both slowly *and* quickly (and certainly not in mere days). This debate is also a question about the existence of power in the Universe of such great ability and magnitude that things beyond our wildest imagination are possible—a power that makes the seemingly impossible, possible. Particle physics, and the humble bumble bee (!), have given us an affirmative answer to the question about the existence of power and ability beyond our present understanding. Mind ignores these inconvenient truths…what about *time,* it ponders? Mind is so heavily invested in its creation of the relative world that it continues to be certain there is no debate it cannot truly win. There must be one truth, it says. Mind believes a choice has to be made between two different perspectives and in an instant, it makes its choice and closes to other possibilities.

From the perspective of the *relative* world, things cannot take a long time and a short time, at the same time. Mind makes a good point. But this is not so from the perspective of the *absolute* – which is how we understand the Universe to be. The Universe—the All-That-Is—is infinite and eternal. Space and time are not as Mind knows them to be—they are without bounds. In the realm of the absolute, there are no divisions, no poles, no this or that. The absolute is without compartments or boundaries. It is without duality. We have seen in the examples just offered, Nature is capable of transcending relativity into the realm of the absolute where polar opposites are indeed possible at the same time. Nature accommodates the *whole* of it. The absolute is complete or whole as it is. The relative is the thing *as it seems*. The absolute is the thing *as it is — or Actual Reality.*

Time is a *relative* concept (as is "space") bound and categorized by man on the Earth plane in order to be better able to wrap his Mind around it all. Man believes that absolute time (i.e., eternity) exists but the reality of eternity boggles his Mind. The Mind of man cannot deal with eternity. Mind cannot *know* eternity. So Mind forgets about eternity and the absolute. The Cosmic Truth about time is that it is neither an event nor a thing and it is not actually measurable i.e., it is not *materially* real. It is a structure created by Mind many years ago. The concept of time is an unavoidable framework of the human mind that preconditions all possible experiences — that is, we set experiences against the backdrop of time. We measure time off in seconds, minutes, hours, or years — all *relative* terms. Relative time is *arbitrary*. Man decided how long to make the unit of time called a minute, and hour, a day or a year.

By partitioning off parts of the whole e.g., minutes or years, we create a manageable, relative concept of time. (Much like we do with the body, assessing and treating it one part at a time in order to try to manage the complexity of all of it.) Man defines time in the relative world to suit him. This makes sense as we are, after all, living in the relative world as long as we are in physical form. Yet this in no way eliminates the fact that on either side of measured time, back of it or ahead of it (we call that "the past" or the "future", also relative terms) is *absolute* time (eternity). In actuality, time is not really a divided thing. The division of time is purely a result of the conscious Mind because our Minds at our current state of evolution or consciousness quite simply cannot know the *whole* of it. The Mind of man in its current state of evolution or unfoldment is *relative*. Therefore, it is unable to grasp the whole of things or the *absolute*, within itself.

We cannot *fully know*, even though Mind may *think* it does, what things may be possible from the perspective of absolute time…like creating the whole world in a "blink of an eye" perhaps? Could evolution of life occur *both* slowly and quickly? Can you expand your conscious Mind enough to even entertain the possibility that *both* perspectives have merit? It is possible that life was created in an instant (or days) *and* in billions of years, depending upon whether you adopt an absolute or relative perspective of time.

All of the descriptors from *both* sides of the debate, Mind's and Nature's, describe the nature of life, *depending upon the perspective from which you view it.* My intent here is to invite you to *transcend duality* in your thinking for just a moment — when it comes to life, the answer to an either/or question can indeed be "both". Step out of the bounds imposed by duality in this relative world of ours. Then look at life free from the limits of Mind's autopilot, *relative* way of thinking. That is the incredible wonder of the human Mind — if you ask it to step out of thinking relatively in the relative world — it can actually do so, at least for the time being! A combined theory of the origin of life merges key concepts from both sides. A combination of both sides takes into account the observations that the planet is ancient and evolutionary processes occur over long periods of time. And it allows for the intuitive sense or faith held by so many people that we are part of something much grander. A unique force which knows no bounds, beyond which is acknowledged or accounted for by conventional science (i.e., Mind's relative concepts), is responsible for the incredible essence we call "life" and for setting into motion the conditions from which life has arisen. Wow! That's interesting (to put it mildly)!

Belief in the foundations of science (Mind) is in no way incompatible with a spiritual perception of things (heart) — especially for those who like to "think outside the box". Likewise, having faith does not rule out reason and reason does not rule out faith — one in no way contradicts or conflicts with the other. Perhaps Einstein said it best:

> *Science can only be created by those who are thoroughly imbued with the aspirations toward truth and understanding. This source of feeling, however, springs from the sphere of religion. To this there also belongs the faith in the possibility that the regulations valid for the world of existence are rational; that is, comprehensive to reason. I cannot conceive of a genuine scientist without that profound faith. The situation may be expressed by an image: Science without religion is lame, religion without science is blind.*

Albert Einstein (1879-1955), Nobel Prize for Physics, 1921

Older (eternal) and more experienced (infinite), Nature has another surprise for Mind up its sleeve. Nature presents an every day example of how we via our Mind can transcend the bounds of time. Our memories are a unique part of us that transcend the constraints of the relative world. Memories get around the impositions of the relative world created by Mind in several ways. There is no material or physical structure of a memory in your Mind. We can stimulate the brain to produce a memory, consciously or electrically, but we cannot examine a neuron and point to a memory contained within it. Memories are *not* of the relative world. They are not *materially* real. They are not observable or measurable. But we know memories to be real. It is just that they are not of this space-time continuum. Memories exist someplace unbound by the Mind-created material or relative world. When asked to retrieve a memory, Mind extends to a higher level of consciousness beyond time as we know it. It reaches into the void and plucks forth a memory. Mind can extend to where the boundary of the relative world we know blurs into the absolute — to the edge of the unbound realms of higher consciousness — to where Mind meets the eternal soul. This is where Mind finds intuition, creative genius and love. These are gifts from the soul to Mind. The higher qualities are unbound by the Mind-imposed rules of the relative world. Like memories, we cannot point to creativity, love, dreams or aspirations either, but we all know them to be real.

We all acknowledge memories are real and memories are ageless. But we might not stop to think that memories are also unbound by time and space. We can send Mind to search for a forgotten memory and suddenly that memory pops in to our conscious awareness out of nowhere. Memory is so automatic, so conditioned, that Mind does not notice itself extending beyond the constraints of its usual, relative world. Mind is an offspring of Nature and as such, it has extraordinary powers. But because Mind is so fixated on and influenced by the relative world that it (along with the five senses) has created, it forgets how extraordinary it is! Unfortunately, Mind tends to forget how extraordinary the rest of the self is too — body and soul are frequently taken for granted or worse, demeaned or diminished. And Mind tends to forget how extraordinary its mother, Nature, is! But we can make a point to "*re*-mind" Mind of all of this!

Is there an every day example of how evolution, also an aspect of Nature, can escape the bounds of Mind's idea of time? There are many examples we commonly hold of evolution behaving in its characteristic slow and linear way. But the evolution of Nature also has the potential to surpass Mind's perceived limits. Over the millennia, gills have gradually evolved into lungs, fins have slowly turned into legs and legs have evolved into wings. But somewhere along that time continuum, Nature gave us the butterfly. After the caterpillar forms a chrysalis, its body parts completely liquefy to feed pre-programmed cells which lie dormant within the caterpillar. In a short period of time, and a quantum leap in evolutionary terms, one small crawling organism literally morphs into another much larger and equally magnificent (assuming you think caterpillars are magnificent—just think of having all of those legs!?) flying organism. Caterpillar life turns into a soup of what appears to be a random or chaotic broth of cells and then reorganizes itself into its next new experience, its next grand version of itself—butterfly life. By one great metamorphosis i.e., from legs to wings in mere days, the caterpillar evolves into its next incarnation of itself. Particles of life are always on their way to becoming something else; only some are in a greater hurry than others.

In tracking the evolution of man, as best as one can do that, we observe many changes in the human body over time including the well-known facts that posture has slowly become more erect and locomotion has shifted to bipedal. We have a less pronounced jaw and smaller teeth. We have developed an opposable thumb, etc. Some of the bits and pieces of man's body have gradually changed over the millennia. But at the same time, another important aspect, the Mind, has evolved not in a gradual, linear fashion as other aspects have, but rather as a *whole*. A change of awareness in one aspect of the Mind transforms the *entirety* of it—the rest of the Mind knows of the change and evolves too at the cellular level. These changes are permanent. That is, the entire Mind evolves with new *awareness* (also referred to as insight). For example, once a young child learns that they can mobilize themselves by crawling and thereby better explore their world, that knowledge transforms their mind at the cellular level and informs their thinking for the rest of their life.

Also, the knowledge acquired by the Mind of one individual can shift permanently the Minds of all men. For example, once man learned that he could make fire—it was not only a revolutionary awareness in that moment—it resulted in an evolution or a quantum leap in the thinking of all men and transformed the way mankind has lived life from that moment in time forward. A shift in thinking, bringing about a new awareness, has the power to transform the Mind and the Mind's experience of life from that moment on.

The evolution of the Mind and the creative intelligence we are capable of proceeds in leaps and bounds, fits and starts—not necessarily linearly and gradually. This fact is reflected in our collective history. If we look at the greatest developments to emerge from the creative intelligence of the Mind of man, we see that progress is marked by long periods of no new substantive developments peppered with sudden bursts or quantum leaps of genius. Evolution can proceed slowly, linearly, predictably, suddenly, unpredictably and dramatically.

And the winner is...

In the final analysis, who is the winner of the Great Debate? What is the nature and origin of life? Does Mind or Nature make the most convincing arguments? What have you decided? Is life planned or random? Inclusive or exclusive? Subjective or objective? For your mind, does one truth apply to life or does the truth of it depend upon perspective? Could both sides of the debate have merit? The point I wish to emphasize here is not just what the answer could be, but the process we go through to find the answers. We accept things we are told if they fit within our comfort zone, our perspective, and reject things that do not. We struggle in our minds to know the truth but we want the truth in the form of *how we understand it*. We can never be open to higher teachings or enlightenment as long as we are *closed to everything except our own truth*. Do not close off the possibility of new truth because you are comfortable with an old one. *Life begins at the end of your comfort zone.*

There are two ways to be fooled. One is to believe what isn't true; the other is to refuse to believe what is true.

Soren Kierkegaard (1813-1855), philosopher

Whoever undertakes to set himself up as a judge of Truth and Knowledge is shipwrecked by the laughter of the gods.

Albert Einstein (1879-1955), Nobel Prize for Physics, 1921

You will decide for yourself what you think about the nature and origin of life, but in the end, life doesn't care! Life does not pick one side to this debate. Life does not espouse to just one truth. Life just keeps flowing—whether you look at it objectively, subjectively, relatively, absolutely, intellectually or intuitively. Both sides of *every* debate are accommodated by life. Life is *all* things. Life is *inclusive*. It is the *whole* of things. Life accommodates all perspectives, all manifestations of it. From the perspective of life, all life forms stand together, equally. And life is always flowing, on its way to becoming something else. If in the moment it seems to be flowing in the direction of randomness or chaos (entropy), it is only temporary for life is on its way to becoming a new, expanded version of itself (evolution). Life knows *its* plan. It is self-organizing and always on its way to becoming the next grand version, without end.

> *The reason why the Universe is eternal is that it does not live for itself; it gives life to others as it transforms.*

> Lao Tzu (approx. 600 BC), philosopher, author of the Tao Te Ching

Man simply cannot *think* his way to answer all questions about life. The mind cannot truly know all of life's mysteries. Nature, the consummate magician, refuses to give up her secrets, which certainly keeps the mind striving for more knowledge and the evolutionary drive advancing. Could that be nature's plan all along? If we knew all the answers to the mysteries of life would the mind start to stagnate? Would entropy set in? Would all of life as we know it eventually cease?

All of life is too vast and too elusive for us to fully comprehend it. Could we just leave it at that and allow for the fact that we do not know everything and simply enjoy the magic and the mystery of life? Let the sacred be sacred? Follow our feelings and intuition and enjoy the journey more? The mind has trouble doing that. Fortunately, we are tri-part beings—mind, body and soul. We are equipped with more than one amazing source of guidance to help us navigate through life and augment our experience of it. Besides the mind, there is also the heart, which speaks to us the wisdom of our soul or spirit.

> *We still do not know one thousandth of one percent of what nature has revealed to us...The most beautiful thing we can experience is the mysterious. It is the fundamental emotion which stands at the cradle of true art and science.*

Albert Einstein (1879-1955), Nobel Prize for Physics, 1921

The debate between Mind and Nature can also be conceptualized as a debate between the *head* and the *heart* where things rational and intellectual i.e., science and the mind's wisdom are on one side, and that which we sense or intuit i.e., heart wisdom (which is the wisdom of your soul—more on this in Chapter Three) and nature, are on the other. The heart is of the natural world, the world of the infinite, the absolute. The capacity of the heart (soul) is unlimited. The mind has its limits. Although the mind is part of nature too, the mind is heavily invested in the relative world because the relative world is an illusion invented by the mind. Because of its investment in this illusion, the mind is prone to moments of insanity. In our hearts, we all know the mind is capable of a great deal of insane thinking and decision making regarding how the mind relates and responds to the rest of humanity and the natural world. The mind takes us away from the heart and nature all too often. The mind chooses to devalue the importance of others and the rest of life all around us. The mind gets caught up in the materialism of the relative world. It gets distracted from the higher values and qualities of the heart. The mind does not always proceed from a perspective of love and benevolence towards the rest of life, or even toward the rest of its own being for that matter. (Just look at what the mind tends to say about the body that houses it.) Heart wisdom is inclusive, allowing, patient, broad, flexible, relaxed, soft and centered. Mind wisdom is prone to being exclusive, critical, perfectionistic, narrow, aggressive, rigid, worried and unstable.

Naturally, we need both the mind and heart (which houses the wisdom of the soul and the wisdom of the natural world). But we need them to work in harmony with each other. Otherwise, we experience an inner conflict which prevents us from flowing with life. If the head and the heart are in conflict, the mind, body and spirit do not function in harmony. This impedes the healthy flow of life's energy through the tri-part being that we are. The energy of the body then becomes blocked or distorted. This results in unhappiness and/or illness and moves us closer to the end of the continuum which is entropy and death as opposed to moving us in the direction of our well-being and growth. Both mind wisdom and heart wisdom (the wisdom of your spirit or soul which comes through to you in the forms of your true feelings and intuition) and "like-mindedness" between the two, play a vital role in our ability to experience a happy, healthy and fulfilled life.

A man is born gentle and weak;
at his death he is hard and stiff.
All things, including the grass and trees,
are soft and pliable in life;
dry and brittle in death.

Stiffness is thus a companion of death;
flexibility a companion of life.
An army that cannot yield
will be defeated.
A tree that cannot bend
will crack in the wind.

The hard and stiff will be broken;
The soft and supple will prevail.

Lao Tzu (approx. 600 BC), 76th verse of the Tao Te Ching

Just as each individual needs to harmonize the different perspectives of the mind and heart in their day-to-day life if they are to have a *good life*, the whole of humanity needs to accommodate both mind and heart wisdom in its processes of decision making and implementation of these decisions if we are to not only survive, but create the circumstances for a *good life for all of life*. The heart plays an essential role in helping the mind to evolve and embrace the higher values. Society's challenge the world over is for the mind and heart of all of humanity and the natural world to coexist in harmony.

In the twenty-first century, we find ourselves in a paradox — the more we advance scientifically and discover the underlying principles of life at work, the more difficulty we have comprehending what our scientific methods have revealed. In other words, the more we know about life, the less we truly understand it! Nature has a sense of humor! As we coax nature to reveal some of her secrets, we realize that the natural world and the Universe we live in are even more mysterious than we thought. The mind can only go only so far in showing us what this mysterious or spiritual quality of life is all about. Reason does not rule out a spiritual quality in all of life. On the contrary, the more we discover through our capacity to reason, the more life reveals its qualities which extend beyond reason to the realm of higher consciousness, the realm of the spirit or soul. The heart is our physical tether in day-to-day life to this higher or spiritual quality, the quality of higher consciousness.

When things seem impossible, unscientific or too far fetched to you — remember, that is exactly what the mind of man first said about such notions as the existence of germs, atoms or black holes, or the possibilities of an automobile powered by a combustion engine, talking on a "telephone", putting a man on the moon, doing math on a "calculator", cooking by "microwaves" or generating power by atomic energy.

Our final decisions are made in a state of mind that is not going to last.

Marcel Proust (1871-1922), author

We are all dismissive (more accurately, frightened) until critical mass is reached and a new idea is commonly accepted. The mind of man fears what it does not know, unlike the heart—this is why we can *feel* our way when we do not *know* the way. The mind of man likes to think it knows all the answers, and in its own mind it does, until eventually *science* proves the mind wrong, time and time again. If we are to uplift all of life on this planet, if we hope to transform and heal humanity, we need to keep reaching with the heart, beyond science as we currently know it, to the higher realms of consciousness. Eventually science catches up with the leap of faith our heart has already made. There are still and always will be higher reaches that science has not yet accessed but that does not have to stop us from aspiring to reach them—*we can reach them with the help of the heart! The power of the heart is unlimited. Heart transcends Mind.*

Ultimately, science needs to find its god in the heart, not the mind. The heart is inclusive and is capable of accessing and entertaining all possibilities—it knows all that the mind knows, and more. It has access to the higher qualities of man including inspiration, creativity, love and benevolence. The heart knows no bounds. However, the mind is limited. The mind is exclusionary. It is prone to making poor choices and frequent painful mistakes which negatively impact life. We need *science* and *spirituality*—the mind and the heart—to join in order to achieve the promise of each, which is to acquire knowledge of the foundations and nature of life not just for the sake of knowing it, but so that we can create going forward a world which is more compassionate and benign for all beings. As our knowledge of the nature of life and our awareness of the interconnectedness of it all increases, so do our responsibilities for our actions towards it. We are our brother's keeper and we are also the guardians and protectors of the so-called lower kingdoms.

Science *and* the soul

Stemming from the centuries-old debate of science versus faith, man has found himself stuck between an either/or choice which somehow feels quite unsatisfactory. It is the mind, not the heart, which says we must choose one or the other — science or the soul. To choose only science feels cold and incomplete. However, to choose only the soul feels uncomfortable as if one is going against our knowledge base. If we were all so pleased with our either/or choice, the mind would not have the need to continue to defend its choice over and over again. This subject would not be the source of such frequent and heated debate or worse. The *uncomfortable feeling* when making an either/or choice is the *wisdom of the heart coming through into the body* which signals that something about this forced choice is indeed not quite right. The truth is we do not have to choose between science and the soul. The belief in *both* does *not go against anything. In fact, trying to separate the two goes against what we now know to be true.*

Science itself gives us a foundation of real evidence to support the existence of the soul i.e., higher levels of consciousness. For that matter, the recent discoveries of quantum physics suggest we need to rethink a lot more than our notions of the soul. Physics now tells us that at its most fundamental level, the entire natural world is not truly understandable in conventional terms. Our conceptualizations of the basics — life, death, health, and the body have not kept up with what *science* has been showing us for over the past century. Physicists have had to dramatically shift their views of reality and life in order to accommodate the extraordinary phenomena they have discovered at the level of atom-life and smaller; however, the general population has *not.* Society's beliefs about these ordinary concepts are based on *old* science. We are reluctant to change our minds because the mind is fearful and does not like to leave its comfort zone.

The 17th Century marked the beginnings of a wide-ranging intellec-tual movement known as the Age of Reason or the Age of Enlightenment. Empiricism and rational thought displaced the religious authority and medieval practices of hypocrisy, corruption, superstition and religious wars which brought suffering and death to countless people. The Age of Reason ushered in sweeping changes with valuable consequences for the modern world including religious freedoms, the application of logic, reason and scientific method and the scientific contributions of Newton and others. Reason and science brought a much needed shift in the way people treated each other, in the way society conducted its affairs (i.e., to move away from the flagrant abusive, illogical and prob-lematic medieval practices), and in the way that people viewed and studied the natural world.

Also, from the changes of the 17th and 18th Centuries came the sep-aration of a host of phenomena including church from state, psyche from soma (mind from body), and body from soul. The practice of separating such things has had pros and cons in the case of the latter two examples. In our efforts to understand these phenomena scientifi-cally, we have embraced the practice of separating natural and whole things into more manageable parts or separate camps. Although this has aided our understanding, we have come to accept these separa-tions and division lines as being real and scientifically based when *they are not.*

Now, in the 21st Century, our focus on things tends to be exclu-sively from the neck up. We have separated the head from the heart. We tend to be preoccupied with all things intellectual. The wisdom and the higher qualities of the other "parts" of us—the soma and the soul, are downplayed or forgotten altogether. Fortunately, science enters the equation once again, this time in the form of quantum phys-ics, to provide some much needed movement back to wholeness, and away from the practice of separating the unique aspects of man into disconnected bits and pieces. The inexplicable, unbelievable, extraordinariness of the ordinary as revealed to us through the window into the world of subatomic particles, actually encourages a shift away from things being all about logic and the mind—which helps to restore *a balanced approach* i.e., a head *and* heart approach to viewing and experiencing life. Modern physics reminds us that we are the whole of it—a mind, body and spirit—and that we are an aspect of a *greater living whole.* There are no unimportant or left-over bits in the Universe. Everything is a vital part of the whole.

The science of the past century confront us with new facts regarding the material or relative world and now things we thought we knew for certain are no longer so. We must admit that there is so much we do not know and there are many phenomena on levels higher which we simply cannot think our way through to arrive at a thorough explanation of them—and yet we cannot deny their existence. The discoveries of physics mark a genuine revolution in our understanding of the world. Our basic ideas of what things really are, where they are, and cause and effect need to be completely revised. There are realms higher and levels of life beyond the intellect and our ability to reason our way through them. Yet the models and theories pertaining to life, medicine, and healing we are currently operating under are at best incomplete, or worse, inaccurate.

Remarkably, recent scientific discoveries actually serve to *put back* some of the mystery and the wonder into our view of life and the human body that some previous scientific discoveries took out. Particle physics reminds us not to make gods of matter and the intellect. Humanity is once again reminded that intuition, feelings and other qualities of the soul, of the higher realms of the non-physical and so-called unprovable, are certainly human qualities as real and essential as the ability to think and reason. In the light of new discoveries, the mind can reunite with the body, and both the mind and the body can reclaim the soul. We can now restore the human being to the incredible *whole* that it truly is.

No matter how wonderful you think your archaeology, your cosmology, your ideology or your theology, there is always room for them to be full of even more mystery and wonder. There are more things about the Universe and who-you-really-are than your mind can possibly know. Watch carefully the mind's tendency to compartmentalize and judge things — especially the tendency to label things as either good or bad, and right or wrong. The mind is relative and is taught the limits of duality and sticks to them out of conditioning or fear. The mind can only define what it already knows and is reluctant to expand to incorporate new information it fears. These characteristics of the mind can narrow life. Fortunately, the amazing mind can also decide to be open to learning something new. Endeavor to expand your mind and broaden your view of life, your view of your body, your view of who-you-really-are. Open your mind and heart to all of life. This helps bring the mind and heart into harmonious alignment. Your body can then benefit from their positive energy. See the magic and the mystery of the life that is all around you and flowing through you. Consciously embrace the higher qualities of the soul e.g., allowance, benevolence, respect and love for all of life, especially for yourself. The best place to start to heal the whole is to heal the part of it that is *you*.

We define our present life and future according to the limited terms of the mind. If you want life to expand more, to bring you desirable variety or change, *change your mind*. Open your mind to something new — for *creation begins with each new thought or idea*.

Human beings are made of body, mind and spirit. Of these, spirit is primary for it connects us to the source of everything, the eternal field of consciousness...We are, in our essential state, pure consciousness. Pure consciousness is pure potentiality; it is the field of all possibilities and infinite creativity. Being infinite and unbounded, it is also pure joy. Other attributes of consciousness are pure knowledge, infinite silence, perfect balance, invincibility, simplicity, and bliss. This is our essential nature. Our essential nature is one of pure potentiality.

Deepak Chopra (1947-), physician, author

The energy and the creative intelligence of the Universe are infinite and you are an aspect of this Source energy. You are the stuff of stars! With a mind open to change and the creative intelligence of the Universe at your disposal—just imagine all the possibilities! There are infinite experiences to be had. There are infinite ways the Universe can bring you what you want, or at least what is in your highest good. There are an infinite number of ways the Universe can answer your question as to how to have a good life. The key is to *ask*, which announces your intent to the Universe. It creates a focal point for energy to operate on. Choosing "what" invites "how" to reveal itself. Then stay open to receiving things *in the way that the Universe (via your soul) brings them to you.* Your soul is not bound by duality. It knows infinite possibilities.

We also define the body according to the limited terms of the mind. What if the truth of the body is completely different than what you have been taught? The body functions as a *whole,* and the sum of its parts does not equal the marvel of the whole of it! Duality is *not* the truth of nature and the Universe. And your body, although it is in the relative world, is in its essence *of* the Universe. You are a child of the Universe—life does not limit you! Your body does not limit you. *You limit you, via your mind.* However, remember that the beauty of the mind is that you can *re*-mind it. So remind yourself that your body channels the same energy and creative intelligence of all of nature, of the entire Universe. You *are* the magic and the mystery of life. What are the possibilities for the health of your body if you keep your mind open to them? Imagine the possibilities, while staying open to the avenues health may come about i.e., not just through matter (e.g., material things), not just through energy (e.g., physical things, such as exercise and eating healthy food), but also through the mind (e.g., your attitudes, beliefs, emotions, thoughts, ideas) and through higher levels of consciousness or spirit (e.g., wholeness, love, intuition, meditation— discussed in Chapter Five).

Despite progress made in the quest to understand it all, and the steps we can take to remind ourselves to keep the mind open, the mind of man quite simply cannot fully grasp the Grand Scheme of it All. The mind of man at its current state of evolution cannot truly and fully know the entirety of the realm of the soul any more than we can truly know the meaning, origin and Source of all life. It is as though there are layers upon layers of veils separating us from knowing or being conscious of the full experience of the grandeur of it all. The realm of the relative is one such veil. Such concepts as higher planes of consciousness, eternity, infinity, an absolute Source of it all and the like literally boggle the mind. It almost physically hurts to try to expand one's thoughts enough in an attempt to truly grasp these notions. These are realms beyond our wildest imagination. The mind tends to discard the ideas that it cannot fully grasp or understand. We say why bother. Or, it is no use. Or, there is no evidence. The intellect may instruct us to dismiss something from a higher plane that it cannot fully know as we cannot see it, measure it, study it, or it just does not fit comfortably into our perspective of things. But this in no way renders it false or non-existent. There is plenty in this world we cannot see and are left to "take it on faith" or theory alone.

Over time, we have gained a great deal of knowledge pertaining to the Mystery of Life and its origins. Also, as our level of consciousness evolves and expands, some of the veils are thrown off and a few rays of wisdom from a higher plane of consciousness beat down upon us. We are currently able to truly know more things formerly thought to be unknowable. Sometimes someone is afforded a glimpse from higher consciousness of great cosmic processes beyond the apparent reality of the here and now. For a fleeting instant they may have a greater sense of the Big Picture; they may know another piece of the Grand Scheme of Things.

You may have known such a moment, perhaps in the presence of the grandeur of nature or in the presence of the ones you truly love. It was as though your mind and heart suddenly opened to a new level and for a moment you transcended time and space and connected with life on a higher plane—on a level of greater love or peace. Perhaps you were moved to tears or could not help but to have exclaimed out loud, "I love life!" It may have been fleeting, but it was undeniably real and out of the ordinary. The wonder of nature and the splendor of love have the power to awaken the higher levels of consciousness within you. Seek them out. Love and peace are two of the qualities of the soul.

Higher "teachings" or so-called "spiritual *knowings*" (including, for example, great creative impulses, moments of genius, intuition and pure love—all of which stem from higher consciousness) are not contrary to the intellect but simply go further "along the continuum" to a higher plane. They do not contradict intellect but simply transcend it. Consciousness is a higher phase, or more refined level of intelligence/thought. From this perspective, consciousness underlies all of life. Consciousness uses its "lower vehicles" (by "lower" I mean less refined, not less important) i.e., mind, energy and matter, as its tools to create the life experience it wishes to create. *You* on a higher plane are a *center-of-consciousness*. *You* are on a journey involving growth and evolution. *You* are on a journey towards an expanded, ever-higher level of consciousness. All of humanity is. And the consciousness that *you* are is *eternal*. Just as matter is an illusion in the material world, so is our concept of time. The consciousness that is who-you-really-are i.e., your soul, transcends the Earth plane and the birth and death cycles of physical matter.

Wholeness

When you step out of the realm of the relative (duality), you open up to the realm of the absolute, also called *wholeness*, which is the realm of infinite possibilities. Actually, it may be more accurate to refer to it as the realm of "all-ness" or "absoluteness", but because those terms are awkward to say, the terms wholeness or oneness are commonly used. Duality (polarity) is limiting because you must choose "one" or "the other". You are locked into a judgment which limits the domain of possibilities to one end of the continuum. This is how the autopilot of most everyone's mind works. But with conscious choice, by asking your mind to be aware of the other possibilities, of the other side of the continuum, you can rise to a higher level or "eagle-eye point of view" in the moment and see the issue from a different perspective. You can then see the *whole* of it, the Big Picture or absolute perspective of it.

The autopilot of the mind, duality, is exclusionary. When you pick one side of things, energy is invested in holding back or holding at bay the other options or possibilities. Duality takes *effort* and creates *resistance* or a block. When a block is created, energy ceases to flow. With duality, which involves judgment, one no longer flows with ease with life. However, from the perspective of wholeness you have no judgment. A perspective of wholeness takes you away from the two extremes of both poles and brings you back to the middle. You stop needing to hold back one end of the continuum. You also stop "swinging" from one pole to the other, which drains energy. Wholeness is in the middle. It is the place where one *transcends* duality; it is where the two poles fuse into *one whole*. This is the place of *allowance*. Wholeness (or oneness) is inclusive. It is about allowance because you *allow* for *all* possibilities—whether or not you agree with them! (Note: Wholeness is allowance, *not* acceptance or agreement. With acceptance, you are in alignment with only one end of the continuum, and you reject or resist the other end.) With wholeness, there are no barriers or resistance as you do not get locked into the limited sphere of one pole. A wholeness perspective sees the entirety of an issue, all of life. Wholeness is unlimited. Wholeness is about *flow*.

Wholeness is inclusive; there is nothing to hold back. The energy of wholeness is the energy of *love*. Wholeness = Love. Love is the synthesis of *all* things. Love is not exclusionary (more on this in Chapter Two). The realm of wholeness or oneness is effortless and creates ease whereby energy can flow. Life flows with ease from this perspective. The energy of wholeness or love is essential for living a happy and fulfilled life and for healing the body (see Chapter Four). The animal and plant world live their lives from the perspective of wholeness and allowance. Animals flow with life. Think of your pet's remarkable ability to go with the flow of what is happening in their daily lives. They do not judge. They do not hold a grudge. They live in the moment. They are so much better at going with the flow than we are! Beyond securing their basic needs for food, shelter and procreation, animals live in wholeness—they take only what they need and *allow* the rest of life to live undisturbed around them. We can learn something from their ways.

Allowing for all possibilities opens your mind, and the rest of you, to vast experiences, an infinite number, actually. Your soul is not bound by relativity or duality. Like nature, your spirit is all about allowing and flowing with ease and joy from all perspectives, through *all* experiences. A shift in consciousness awareness to a wholeness or loving perspective on things produces a shift not only in your mind but in your *body as well.* A new awareness or information that you become conscious of can have a powerful impact on the rest of your tri-part being. For example, notice how your entire being is impacted the moment you are aware of someone criticizing you. You will experience a shift in all parts of you—how you think, feel and at the cellular level (heart rate, blood pressure etc.). Now notice the impact in your being when you are aware of yourself or someone else sending you love. *Awareness (which is a form of information) is a form of energy. It has the power to move you.* The energy of wholeness or love is the strongest power of all. It has the power to move you to the heights of happiness, fulfillment and good health. We are mind, body and spirit. A shift in the energy of any one aspect of your tri-part being will affect the other aspects of *you.*

In summary, there is a universality of all life

This book invites you to shift your perspective and expand your awareness of what it means to be alive, how you view the rest of life all around you, how you view your journey through life and how you view your physical body. See what helpful shifts a new perspective, an expanded awareness, can bring to your experience of daily life. For maximum joy and health in living, wellness needs to be facilitated at every level—mentally, physically and spiritually—including your outlook on life. See your uniqueness, the marvel that you really are, as well as your connectedness to all of life in the Big Picture. It is time for a fresh beginning. Look at life through new eyes and fall in love with yourself and all of life again!

We have established that everything in the material world shares, at a fundamental level, a common structure and a common supply, literally. The atoms of your physical body are fresh from the vast virtual "Store House" of all energy particles and will quickly return to it again. The constant exchange of atoms in your body results in a new skeleton every three months, new skin every month and a new stomach lining every four days. That which is part of your flesh today may have been part of an animal or plant a few days before, and may be part of some other living person or thing a few days from now. Wow! In the paradoxical nature of life, change is the one constant. From the perspective of the Grand Scheme of Things, you do not own one atom of matter *personally*. What is yours today was someone else's yesterday and will be still another's tomorrow. Your soul is the only part of you that is unique to you and enduring. You draw upon the Source of all energy particles every moment of your life, taking what you need and then allowing it to pass on. This Source is present everywhere, at all times, linking all of life. Every particle of life is one bit of the common supply, one drop from the great ocean of omnipotent intelligent energy that flows through you and all of life at the same time, on and on forever.

At the fundamental level, all of life is formed from the same basic building block, the same intelligent energy. Hence the well known expressions, "We are all one with life." And, "All of life is one." This is the universality of life. Every different thing, vibrating to its own "tune", pulsating with its own heartbeat, appears different on the surface as it unfolds and expresses its unique qualities. Every thing is unique and apparently separate, yet all has its roots in the Source, rendering it inseparable from the Source of it all. All of life is one. All of life has value and is an integral and vital part of the Big Picture.

Charles Darwin gave us the concepts of the interrelatedness and interdependence of all species in his seminal work, *On the Origin of Species*, published in 1859. The results of his genetic studies produced a quantum leap in humanity's perception of life on Earth. (Incidentally, he delayed publication of his manuscript for 15 years out of fear for his life. The notion of the transmutation of species was not acceptable by the mainstream in the 1840's.) Darwin considered it absurd to talk of one form of life as being superior to the other. He noted that while the human would view the development of the intellect as the key indicator of evolutionary achievement, bees would chose instincts as the criterion. Darwin's adoption of a non-human orientation to life on Earth was an enormous break in the conventional wisdom and theology of the day.

Our present knowledge of genetics reveals just how interrelated all of life truly is. You may be familiar with the oft-cited statistic that the human being shares over 99% of his/her genetics with the chimpanzee. But did you know that you share 90% of your genes with a mouse and 60% with a banana?! (Thank you to Deepak Chopra for citing those rather startling and humbling facts!)

Expand your concept of what it means to be *alive*. Regard life every where as the bit of intelligent energy that it is. This intelligence is alive. Make no mistake. There is no such thing as a dead, unintelligent Universe. You are not atoms of life, floating on a sea of death. You are atoms of life surrounded by a pulsating, vibrating, moving, *thinking* sea of life. All of matter is alive. There is no such thing as dead matter. Every particle has energy, intelligence and a life force. Everything is ensouled, endowed with a drop of the Source of it all. Look around you to the animal, plant, insect and yes even the mineral world and all you see is life, life, life and more life. There is no true void, no left over bits, no useless or lowly parts. *You are part of a Living Whole.* Make a commitment to take a more reverent and benevolent approach to all of life for no thing in life is insignificant, and every thing in life wants *a good life.*

 Honor the sacred
Honor the Earth, our Mother
Honor the Elders
Honor all with whom we share the Earth:
Four-leggeds, two-leggeds, winged ones,
Swimmers, crawlers, plant and rock people.
Walk in balance and beauty.

Native American Elder, author unknown

Wake up to the *absolute miracle* that is *you* and *everything* that is living all around you. You do not need to look beyond everyday life to find miracles. They are here now — walking, hopping and crawling beside you, flying through the air above you, swimming near you, growing in your garden. You need not look any farther. Your miracles are already here — the wonder and marvel of *you* and of the experience of your daily life on Earth with all its contrasts are the miracles *you* have been seeking.

There are two ways to live: you can live as if nothing is a miracle; you can live as if everything is a miracle.

Albert Einstein (1879-1955), Nobel Prize for Physics, 1921

If we could see the miracle of a single flower clearly, our whole life would change.

Buddha (563-483 B.C.), philosopher, sage, mystic

Expand your concept of who-you-really-are. Know that you and your body are a truly incredible manifestation of matter, energy, intelligence and consciousness. You are consciousness presently focused on having a physical life. You are not a physical being leading a spiritual life, but rather a spiritual being living a physical life, for a brief time. Awaken to the higher qualities of your soul! Live a more conscious, awakened life now, in the present moment, and for the duration of time that you occupy your amazing body. Do not sleepwalk through it all!

You need not wait for your ship to come in. Your journey has already started—whether you get on the boat or not! One of your challenges in this lifetime is to remember to enjoy the trip. So, make a point to *be present*, on purpose. Make a point to remember to enjoy it all, starting right now! Your soul knows how wonderful, how absolutely delicious all of your life is and never stops its attempts to awaken your mind to this. Your soul, your source of higher guidance, is what inspired you to read this book—just one of the ways it "talks" to you all the time. Your soul is on a journey to enlightenment—so lighten up, literally! Open your mind and heart to hold more of your soul's light.

Chapter Two

LIFE ON PLANET EARTH

From the Big Picture perspective, it's all about growth and expansion

*Y*ou are so much more than you think you are! You are a center-of-consciousness, a spirit or soul manifest in physical form. The conscious intelligence that you are, your soul, uses its tools i.e., your mind and your physical body, to unfold who-you-really-are (the essence of which is a drop from the Source) on the Earth plane. You are Source energy and you are a creator! You are on Earth to create and experience the *physicality* of life. The marvel of the physical body enables you to sense and feel in all ways physically possible the material world — up close and personal. An endless array of sights, sounds, tastes and textures await your senses here. The incredible variation in nature i.e., the animal and plant life around the world supports the whole process of our experiencing and creating diversity. Our life experiences and creations are influenced and expanded by observing and being inspired by the fantastic forms of life nature shows us.

You are an eternal being comprised of physical, emotional, mental and spiritual energies which allow you to participate in the creation of the All-That-Is. You have chosen at this time to focus an aspect of the consciousness that you are into physical form on the Earth plane — on the cutting edge of creation. In so doing, you will evolve and the All-That-Is will evolve through you. At the same time, a broader, wiser, eternal aspect of you continues to span the heights of higher consciousness, the soul plane.

Through our eyes the Universe perceives itself. Through our ears the Universe is listening to its harmonies. We are the witness through which the Universe becomes conscious of its glory, of its magnificence.

Paraphrase of the writing of Alan Watts (1915-1973), philosopher

With the myriad of different experiences life on Earth brings, in fact *because of* the endless variation on life's themes that you could possibly experience, *you* chose to be here. You could not wait to get here! The consciousness that is uniquely you, your soul or "eternal self", knew that your life experiences, however short or long, seemingly positive or negative, would result in your growth. At the level of consciousness, the soul plane, you *never* forget this. *You* never lose track of your mission to amass experiences and to grow. The wonderful diversity (including the negativity) of the Earth plane, the leading edge of creation, provide the opportunity to enable you to form opinions and desires about how life could be improved. The contrasts of the physical world, the world of duality, enable you to define a better experience and help you choose what to create next. Through your desires and creations, not only is an expanded *you* created, but an expanded world is created. When life on the physical plane expands, life on the non-physical plane i.e., consciousness, expands.

> *Just by being ourselves we are borne toward a destiny far beyond anything we could imagine. It is enough to know that the being I nourish inside me is the same as the Being that suffuses every atom of the cosmos.*

Deepak Chopra (1947-), physician, author

For the Universe and for life on planet Earth, expansion and evolution is what it is all about. And, in the Big Picture of your life, it is no different. You are a creator. You are an experience-seeking being. You are a growth-seeking being. You are on a continuous evolutionary journey to higher, expanded levels of consciousness. Growth is in *your highest good.* From the perspective of your soul, *everything* that happens to you is in your highest good as it will contribute to your growth and expansion in the long run. And your soul is indeed in it for the long run. The consciousness that is *you* has eternity to achieve its goals—to create, conceive and experience all that it wishes to. In so doing, you will evolve. And in so doing, you will become the next grand and glorious version of who-you-really-are.

From the perspective of the Earth plane and your physical body, in the absence of growth, there is decay. There is a driving force underlying all of life. A force constantly "pulls" at life to keep it forever moving. Life builds up, grows and flourishes, or it breaks down, declines and disintegrates. There is either growth or entropy. Nothing in life stands still or stagnates—not the energy that comprises your body, not the energy that is an apple on the tree, not the energy that is the rock in your garden. You can actively facilitate your growth and flourish, or you can allow the forces of entropy to wear on you prematurely. Yes, sooner or later your body gives way then gives out—but you can influence the speed at which you approach a given end of the con-tinuum! You can nurture your quality of life and the health of your body. Perhaps man's life span and state of health are limited more by his beliefs than by *anything* else.

Opportunities for you to create and experiences for your growth and expansion will flow to you continuously throughout the duration of your physical life on this planet. The events of your life result in your evolution. You can be alert to this, look for them and make a point of consciously facilitating the process, or you can more or less sleepwalk through it all. Given the awe-inspiring wonder and incredible beauty of life all around you, wouldn't it be a crying shame to sleep through some of it, any of it? That is not what the conscious intelligence that is *you* had in mind when it materialized as you on Earth! Sadly, sleep-walking through life is what so many people do.

In the absence of an existential or Big Picture perspective of oneself and the journey of life, it can be very difficult to hang onto a sense of purpose and meaning in the face of the demands of daily living. By midlife, it is not unusual for people to feel as though they are just sur-viving rather than living a joyous life. Have you been feeling that way lately? Would you describe yourself or your life using such phrases as: you feel like something is missing from your life; you cannot seem to get motivated; you are just going through the motions; you find your-self worrying about every little thing; you do not feel like your usual self; you feel exhausted, overwhelmed, stuck or dissatisfied? If these feeling are enduring, with the addition of another stressor (and it may not take much to tip the scales at this point), this midlife or existential crisis can grow into a full blown depression, anxiety disorder and/or it can manifest in somatic complaints or chronic disease. Depression and anxiety have become alarmingly common problems. Professional psychological help is recommended at this stage, preferably before. Do not wait until things are at their worst to do something about them. Seek help to support and guide you. Hopefully, you will be inspired to find a pathway towards positive change in this book.

As life progresses, we tend to forget that we are here as a tri-part being—a mind, body and soul—to conceive, create and experience all that life has to offer. We get off balance by ignoring or failing to nurture one or more of our vital aspects. We judge harshly and abuse the body terribly. We forget that we are here to experience the physicality of life through the amazing wonder of the body. We fail to develop our mental potential. We do not nurture the soul or listen to its guidance (i.e., our true feelings and core values). We get off track or stuck on "autopilot" and we forget to embrace the many qualities of the soul—play, fun, creativity, wisdom, laughter, empathy, compassion, love and more. We forget to value and nurture the entirety of our *being*. When that happens, the mind, body and soul do not function in harmony. We do not flow with ease and joy in life. Growth stagnates and we are vulnerable to the forces of entropy. Pain and/or illness may develop.

You can choose to be more aware

You can go through life consciously or unconsciously, aware or unaware, awake or asleep. Besides missing out on so many opportunities for experience that life would like to offer you, navigating through life unaware or on autopilot eventually produces a meaningless, dissatisfying, difficult life, or worse, a depressed and painful daily existence where life no longer feels worth living. In living without awareness, life stops expanding and starts pulling back in on itself. Growth stops. Entropy starts.

The higher qualities of the soul and the wisdom which permeates the body will remind us of the meaning, purpose and joy of life if we remember to listen to it. Being more conscious or aware in life can alert you to opportunities to create and experience things so that you do not let them pass you by. Also, being more aware of your mission here to learn and grow can help you to get through things that you are not happy about. For example, being alert to a learning or growth potential embedded in a problematic pattern repeating in your life can help you to get through it by mobilizing you to do something about it. When you "get" the learning the problematic pattern stops repeating. You move on to the next experience or next great opportunity.

Also, the conscious reminder to yourself that you are an experience-seeking being can help to ease you through the things you do not want but cannot do anything about. In the face of being unable to change or resolve something, you are left with the choices of *resisting* it or *allowing* it. Doing your best to *allow* it would, for example, mean adopting an attitude of "well, this is *interesting*…" Or, "This is *some* experience I am collecting along my journey!" An attitude of allowing can help you to *go with the flow* of what you do not want and before long, flow right out of it. You are less likely to get caught up in the upset of it. While not easy, it may be the best you can do in the moment. You may be familiar with the expression, "What you resist, persists!"

The really happy person is one who can enjoy the scenery when on a detour.

Anonymous

You, *on the soul plane,* created who you are at the outset of this physical life that you chose to have. While we are living it, we sometimes forget how great it is to be in a physical body and experiencing the physicality of this planet. Allow me to remind you of some of the simple pleasures. When was the last time you really enjoyed, I mean with *full conscious awareness*: the sun on your skin; the sensation of warm water flowing all over you in the shower; the scent of freshly ground coffee beans; the color of fall leaves; the song of birds in the spring; the taste of your favorite indulgence; the thrill of creating something new in your life; great sex; the spark of light in your loved one's or beloved pet's eyes …and on and on it goes. *You* must have thought it was great to be on Earth or you would not have chosen to be here!

There is always more that your soul would like to create and experience and that life would like to offer you. Imagine all that you could experience if you switch off the "autopilot" *and* step out of the limits of *relative* thinking. Are your habitual thoughts limiting you? Do any of these sound familiar: it can only be this way or that way; there is only this or that solution; I can never do that; I must always do this; this is all there is? *Life does not limit you. You limit you.* There are limitless ways you can experience your heart's desires if you stay alert to opportunities for change, ask for what you want, and stay open to the *way* life would like to give you what you are asking for. It may not always come to you exactly the way you wanted, but it will always come in the way of your highest good.

Make a vow right now to not let any more of life just pass you by. Wake up! Stay alert! Make a point of being more *aware* in your day-to-day life. Unplug society's electronic umbilical chords more often (TV, cell phone, computer, ipod etc.) and plug into your relationships and your physical environment *directly. Aim to be in the moment with your full conscious attention.* Spend more time in the quiet solitude of nature (without) and the peaceful stillness which envelopes the higher levels of you (within) on a regular basis. Make a point of switching off the autopilot and being consciously aware of the ways that life is unfolding all around you and how you are creating the experiences your mind and soul wishes to have. When you are fully conscious moment-to-moment in the life that you have created, you are better able to make changes and create more of what you are wanting. You can work on what you are conscious of. You cannot work on what you are not conscious of!

Embrace the situations unfolding in your life and be willing to learn from them and unfold your full potential. Encourage your growth processes, not stagnation, which quickly gives way to deterioration. Evolution proceeds *through* you, with or without your conscious awareness of it. Do not let another day of your evolution proceed without your being aware of it and having a say in it!

 Life is what happens to you while you're busy making other plans.

John Lennon (1940-1980), musician, song writer

 May you live all the days of your life.

Jonathan Swift (1667-1745), author

While in a physical form, we forget who-we-really-are. And we do not have conscious memory of the manifestation of life that we were before the current experience in material life. You may be thinking, "I did not create my life for I would not have chosen *this!*" But *you* — as a result of the activity of your soul and mind — did. (Note: We never really know which aspects of our life have been created by which aspects of ourselves—soul or mind. This is one of the Great Mysteries of Life. I have heard of life's journey being described in the following way. Imagine you are riding down the beach perched on top of two galloping horses, one foot on the back of each, with the reins in your hands. You do not know which horse you can steer and which one you can't. You are left to do your best to direct them both where you want to go as you are speeding along, and to enjoy the ride!) You continue to create your life from day to day—from the perspective of your physical self, and from your non-physical self on a higher plane of consciousness. You, via your soul and mind are engineering your life.

You can *facilitate* (but not control totally) the process of change and create something new through your conscious awareness and intent—i.e., your thoughts and actions. (Your soul will have intentions that your mind does not know about.) If something is happening in your life which is not to your liking, imbedded somewhere in it is an opportunity for you to learn, make a change (in your thoughts and/or behavior), grow and move on. Look for the learning.

Earth is a planet of dualities

Earth is the ideal fertile ground from your soul's perspective as it offers an infinitesimal variety of life, stimuli, and circumstances from which you can experience, learn and grow. This relative world, or world of duality, provides a backdrop for everything which enables you to make comparisons between things. That is, for every manner of things here, there is a polar opposite to it—something so very different from it or on the opposite end of the continuum. Duality (or polarity) provides a frame of reference enabling us to compare something against it, thereby understanding what we are experiencing.

For example, how do we really know what the experience of light is unless we have experienced darkness? How do we know what heat feels like unless we have felt cold? How do we know what abundance is unless we have experienced lack? Without the contrasts that duality provides, we could not get the understanding and the experience of the physicality of life that we came here to get. On the Earth plane, in the relative world, everything is *relative* to or *in contrast* to everything else. All states are relative to their opposite, enabling us to understand the meaning of it. Dark and light, tall and short, hard and soft, loud and quiet, satiation and hunger, happiness and sadness, strong and weak, beauty and ugliness — we are on a planet of duality or opposite charges.

All things in the relative world bring pros and cons. Even duality has pros and cons. The frame of reference of duality is vital to our ability to make contrasts and thereby understand things. And yet duality limits our perspective. We tend to loose sight of the entire continuum of possibilities and see or experience only the two poles or charges. Also, we get caught up in judgment and label one pole as good, the other as bad.

There is no escaping duality as long as you are living on this planet. However, taking a "break" from it in your mind is good for the tri-part being that you are — it provides a rest from the mental and emotional "swinging back and forth" that it creates. Such a rest is healing and restores balance between the body, mind and spirit. As described in Chapter One, you can momentarily transcend duality in your thinking when you go to the perspective of *wholeness*. Here you rise above the perspective of relativity and the two poles are seen as equally charged points along a vast continuum — they are not good or bad, they just *are*. From a wholeness perspective, there is no judgment. From this position of higher consciousness, one *allows* for all possibilities and can go with the flow of life as it twists and turns. It can be quite useful to remind yourself to take a wholeness perspective as often as you can.

Life is made up of positive and negative charges in perfect balance

Everything in life is composed of the equal and opposite energy or charge, whether you are looking at the Small Picture (e.g., atoms or molecules) or the Big Picture of life (e.g., a given event or facet of life in general, such as relationship well-being, occupational well-being, financial or physical well-being). *The positive and negative charges always balance out.* Just as the chemical composition of matter consists of balanced charges, *so does the very fabric of your life.* Overall, your life really is a *balanced equation!* The more the charge or energy of a situation is skewed to one end of the continuum, the sooner the opposite charge will appear (in the same facet or in a different one). And, it will come with sufficient strength to balance the *overall* equation of your life. Wow! This is a phenomenal assertion which is hard to believe. But this theory is supported upon further scrutiny — despite any objections your *mind* may be generating at this very moment. Open your mind to this new idea, and then see what you think of it.

Take any given situation in life, labeling for the moment, the positive end of the continuum as "good" and the opposite or negative end as "bad". When you are feeling something is good, there is always the potential for the opposite end of the continuum to present or express itself. That is, something you are not happy about will sooner or later occur. Such is life on the planet of duality! Life brings an equal and oppositely charged experience into our life to *balance* us. The "charge" of your life equation is *always* moving in the direction needed to bring your life back to balance, even if it does not appear to be at first glance. Consider the specific example of winning cash in a lottery. This event is commonly held to be a so-called positively charged or desirable event. Being given a load of cash would be considered a really great thing by most people. However, winning the lottery also contains the equal and opposite *potential*. Inevitably, the strongly negative side of the equation — e.g. harassments from others wrangling for money, hard feelings, fears of losing it, etc. — will emerge. The negative side will present itself with equal strength as the positive until your life is balanced. Or, the lottery win may bring more positives than negatives, but then another facet of life brings sufficient negative charge to balance the *overall* equation of your life. You win the lottery but you lose friends. Your financial life goes well, but your social or family life goes poorly. In the long run, the energy that is your life is a perfect balance of positive and negative charges.

In the same way, so-called bad or negative events carry the equal and opposite potential for positive charges. For example, it is not uncommon to hear someone say that losing their job turned out to be the best thing that could have happened to them. The loss of the job was balanced by the development of a good new opportunity for work. Or the job may have been lost, but the soul mate was found. Or, the occurrence of something unwanted (the negative charge) was balanced out by learning a helpful life lesson (the positive charge) which led to personal growth. Life acts to balance the overall equation of one's life. The closing of one door necessitates the opening of another for the positive and negative charges must balance.

When one door closes another door opens; but we so often look so long and so regretfully upon the closed door, that we do not see the ones which open for us.

Alexander Graham Bell (1847-1922), inventor

The positives will present themselves in the face of the negatives, a fact which has given rise to the well known expressions, "Make a silk purse out of a sow's ear." "Find the treasure in the trauma." And, "Every problem has a gift for you in its hands." Take stock in the central areas or facets of your life — physical, emotional, relational, occupational, financial and spiritual. If you make a thorough examination of all areas, you will find the pluses and minuses balance out overall. Stay alert to the potential for learning and growth. The positives will arrive to counterbalance the negatives, only perhaps not quite in the way in which you expect. However, the positive and negative experiences will always balance out.

Duality results in emotional swings

The more you accumulate a given charge, the more the energy of the situation is skewed to one side. This will quickly attract the opposite side of the equation, i.e., an oppositely charged situation will soon materialize. You will then have a time when you are having the opposite experience or feeling the opposite emotional reaction until your entire life reads like a balanced equation. Before long, the pattern will repeat all over again. *No one can have only a positively charged life. Equally, no one is having only a negatively charged life. That is fantasy or illusion. It is an illusion caused by duality.*

Some believe that depression is what results when life is not living up to one's fantasy of how it "should be" i.e., all or mainly positives. The illusion of an unequal positive to negative ratio is created by our judgments and feelings. How we *feel about or react to* the two ends of the poles could be predominantly positive or negative depending on the particular situation and the personality of the individual. However, both ends of the scale are always embedded in life experiences whether you notice them, feel them, or not. There may be an *appearance* of a life skewed to the positive or skewed to the negative, but from an energy perspective, your life is a balanced equation.

All of nature aims for equilibrium. From the perspective of the soul plane, you and everyone else is leading a perfectly balanced life. And, all that is happening in your life is coming about in the *perfect* way to aid your growth perfectly well. In other words, all that is happening to you is in your highest good. Human beings judge and label the ends of the poles with *emotional* charges or values. We say something is desirable, good, right or undesirable, bad, wrong — according to our experience and teachings. Judging things is an inevitable part of the experience of being human and we all do it. However, by adopting the perspective of *wholeness*, the polarity drops away. Daylight is not "good" and nighttime "bad". Hot is not "good" and cold "bad". Tall is not "right" and short is not "wrong", etc. *In their essence*, these states are not good or bad, right or wrong, *they just are*. They are simply parts of the whole, or points along a continuum. They are part of the All-That-Is. From the perspective of the All-That-Is, which is the same as saying the perspective of wholeness (or the absolute), there is no polarity. There is no judgment.

We typically judge or label things instantly (a reaction of the mind), based on our learning, understanding, and teachings which include societal influences. Also, our *true* emotional reactions, which are hard-wired (which come via the soul), result in our just instantly feeling how we feel about things. (Emotions are discussed in more detail in Chapter Three.) With the positives and negatives of life coming at us all the time, our emotions end up swinging back and forth all the time. We swing from — this feels good and I am happy — to this feels bad and I am unhappy. The swing changes direction from moment to moment, sometimes even from thought to thought. The bigger the charge of the situation, the bigger the oppositely charged situation will be. For those who tend to experience life in a dramatic way, their swings will be bigger. Big swings mean experiences of dramatic emotional highs and elated moods, to melodramatic emotional lows. You could argue that bigger is better, but bigger can also be more draining. There are pros *and* cons to the big and small swings of emotionality — what else would you expect from the planet of duality?!

As you well know, this is how daily life goes from an emotional perspective. For example, the picnic is "good" (swinging to one pole now) but the ants on the blanket are "bad" (swinging to the other now, unless you happen to really like the ants, in which case something else that you do not like will eventually show up, such as tuna salad sandwiches, unless you like tuna, then a thunderstorm might show up to rain you out, unless you happen to really like thunderstorms, in which case…) and on it goes. The roses are beautiful (swing) but the thorns are ugly (swing). The color of this shirt is right (swing), but the cut is wrong (swing). I like this cereal (swing), but I do not like the raisins in it (swing). Our emotions swing back and forth between the two poles day in and day out, moment to moment. There is no escaping duality. But, *who-you-really-are does not want to escape it. You* chose to be on the plane of duality, which includes negativity in equal measure. Why do we need negativity?

Negativity serves an important purpose

There is a strong propensity of the mind to maintain that a perfect life, meaning all positives and no negatives, *can* be obtained. The mind tells you that you can and truly will achieve the perfect life when…or if only…you find your soul mate, you can afford your dream home, you get the right job, you loose 20 pounds… etc. Duality means judgment. The mind judges the negatives, well, negatively! It does not want the negatives. The mind imagines and believes in a life without them.

However, nature, in her infinite wisdom (and your soul) knows that a life without negatives would not be optimal for growth and evolution.

Character cannot be developed in ease and quiet. Only through experience of trial and suffering can the soul be strengthened, ambition inspired, and success achieved.

Helen Keller (1880-1968), author

Is suffering really necessary? Yes and no. If you had not suffered as you have, there would be no depth to you, no humility, no compassion.

Eckhart Tolle (1948-), author

And as you know, growth and evolution is what it is all about here on Earth. Nature ensures that conditions are optimal for evolution. And conditions for evolution are optimized when life offers an equal balance of both sides of the equation. Duality is necessary for evolution, therefore nature ensures conditions and situations on Earth are not one-sided. If only the positive or only the negative side of the continuum presented itself, a vast limit would be imposed on the possibilities life could bring. We would be limited to life experiences from only one-half of the equation. While this might appeal to you on the Earth plane (as long as you got the positive half!), your soul never forgets its goal of growth and expansion. The presence of any limiting factor is not optimal for maximum growth so life obligingly provides experiences from both ends of the scale.

Also, if we experience something we find to be negative or undesirable, we are inspired or pushed to do something about it. Negative experiences catapult us forward, thereby facilitating our growth. You are no doubt familiar with the expression, "That which does not kill you makes you stronger."

I'm not afraid of storms, for I'm learning to sail my ship.

Louisa May Alcott (1832-1888), author

We are problem-solvers. We are creators. We are growth-seeking beings and negativity is a powerful motivator for growth and creative processes. If everything was blissful, would you even want to get out of bed? There would be no problems to solve, nothing pressing that needed your attention. Everything could wait. If nothing annoyed you, if you had no concept of "this is worse than that" or "this is better than that", you would not make any changes. You would not create anything new. You would not be able to define and create a *better* experience, thereby improving on the status quo and *lifting life up* to a higher level. And, as you will recall, in the absence of creation there is stagnation—expansion stops, entropy starts and eventually life ceases to be.

Also, without a balance of negativity, it would take forever to decide to do anything, even the simplest of things. For example, imagine if there was no polarity, no negatives, no "this is worse than that" or "this is better than that" and you were trying to decide what to wear. It might go something like this: What shall I wear today? I think I will wear my blue shirt. I really like my blue shirt. It is great. But here is my green shirt next to it, hmmm. I really like my green shirt. It is just as great as the blue one. So, shall I wear my green shirt today? But here is my blue shirt next to the green one, hmmm. I really like my blue shirt. It is just as great as the green one, hmmm. What shall I wear today? Life would not expand very quickly at this rate and neither would your growth. It might take you a full lifetime just to decide which shirt to wear!

We are in physical form to create and experience the physicality of life, an important aspect of which is cause and effect. Because we experience positives *and* negatives, when we do something, we are able to evaluate the results of our actions and learn. This enables us to evolve in the direction of our core values, i.e., we grow according to the wisdom of our consciousness or soul. And the non-physical aspect of ourselves has the benefit of the expansion that we gain from the physical experience (this aspect is ever-expanding to higher and higher levels of consciousness). We learn because a given outcome is *relative* to another possible outcome. (E.g., If I do "x", then "y" gets better. If I fail to do "a", then "b" gets worse.) Without both the negatives and positives, our growth would not progress and life would stagnate. In the absence of negativity, the status quo would be maintained. Life is not about maintaining the status quo. It is about change. It is about evolution, not stagnation and entropy. Life cannot sustain itself under the latter conditions. Our beings crave change and growth, even if we (our minds) are afraid of it sometimes.

To experience what life offers to the maximum, to learn and grow the maximum possible amount in this lifetime, you need the impact of the whole continuum, not just half of it. You need duality. You need contrast. You need negativity. You need the whole enchilada! You need it all in order to know what you want to create more of, and what you want less of. This is why you chose to be here. This is part of the creating, learning, growing, expanding process. Sorry, but just like the vegetables you do not like, those negatives are good for you too—they give you the opportunity to grow. On the planet of duality, the negatives are both negative and positive—another paradox courtesy of Mother Nature!

Life eventually exposes us to the All-That-Is in order for us to grow and expand in every possible way. The All-That-Is would not be the *All*-That-Is without both ends of the continuum, it would only be the

Half-That-Is, only part of the potential of the All-That-*Could*-Be, which is what the All-That-Is is about to become! Creation, expansion, evolution—this is what *you* are all about. That is what life is all about. That is what the Universe is all about—forever evolving through you and everyone else.

Step off the swing as often as you can

Duality, providing contrasts everywhere we look, everywhere we go, has a powerful influence on how we *experience* daily life on this planet. As a result, our emotional reactions to the positives and negatives of life change continuously. Emotions swing between the positive and negative poles of things with each passing event, or even each passing thought. Feelings swing back and forth day to day, hour to hour, or even minute to minute depending on what is going on. One moment we're happy; the next, we're sad. We like this; now, we don't. We want something else. We're up. Now, we're down. Being human means experiencing the emotional swings resulting from polarity/contrast for as long as we live. Sounds tiring, doesn't it? While there is no escaping duality (and the consciousness that is *you* does not want to), one thing starts to become glaringly obvious, living a physical life on a planet with duality, judgments and emotional swings can be exhausting! We need *revitalizing* on a regular basis! The tri-part being that you are needs a break, an opportunity to rest, regenerate and revitalize. And how do you do that? This section outlines some steps you can take to help you do just that.

It is crucial to pay attention to what you think about. Remember, creation happens from the *top down.* That is, from higher vibration to lower vibration—from thought to energy (vibrating at a slower speed than thought) to physical matter (energy in a slower vibration still). Positive thinking is very important. Thoughts are *active* within you. They create vibrations or electrical activity in the body. Thoughts and emotions translate into bodily electrical impulses, which in turn impacts body chemistry and cellular activity. *Beliefs create chronic vibrational patterns.* They impact health and well-being more than we realize. Also, by the Cosmic Law of Attraction (i.e., that which is like unto itself is drawn — or to put it another way, like attracts like), a given energy vibration will attract more of the same energy. Another way to say this is by the expression, "You get what you think about or focus on — even what you don't want, if what you don't want is what you are focusing on." So, *keep your focus on what you want as best as you can.*

Thinking positively as often as you can is always a good idea and we all have a choice as to where to put our focus. Maintaining your focus on what feels good and on what is wanted as often as possible will result in your *experiencing the contrasts of life more positively, more often.* (Nevertheless, the contrasts will still be there.) After all, you did not come here to feel badly in the life you chose. That makes no sense. You came here to enjoy the process of creating, experiencing and expanding and you knew you needed contrast for that — contrasts are an integral part of the creation process. Making a point to be more consciously aware of your style of thinking and keeping it as positive as possible is likely to help move you through an unwanted feeling or situation more rapidly. Try to keep your focus on what is right about your life, not on what is wrong. And focus on what is right about your body, not on what is wrong with it. Because there is so much more right *to experience* about the physicality of life than wrong!

Happiness is not having what you want; it is wanting what you have.

Anonymous

> *Joy is what happens when we allow ourselves to recognize how good things are. Joy is not necessarily what happens when things unfold according to our plans.*

Marianne Williamson (1952-), author

How can you rest and regenerate from the inevitable duality/contrast swings that life brings? Start by seeking out as many moments as you can where you can "get off the swing". I mean throughout the day, while you are *awake*. Time spent sleeping is not enough to replenish your body and restore a balance between mind, body and soul. Your being requires *more* than sleep alone. You need to spend some time with a quiet mind (at least relatively quiet, for we are always thinking) and in peaceful communion with your body and surroundings in order to come back to equilibrium and facilitate healthy functioning in your body. *This is vital to achieving maximum wellness.*

Seek out opportunities to be still, alone and quiet. Being still and quiet (i.e., stop *doing* and just *be,* or be a human *be-ing!*) is *nourishing to your entire being, and your being needs this on a regular basis.* It fosters a *wholeness* frame of mind. This can take the form of simply sitting still and being quiet for a while, taking time to reflect, or meditating (or walking slowly and focusing on the environment around you, i.e., a walking meditation). (Meditation is discussed in greater detail in Chapter Four.) Meditation is about slowing down and *allowing* your thoughts i.e., releasing judgment which results from polarity. In stillness and quiet you leave judgment behind and move into allowing All-That-Is. Recall from Chapter One, the state of allowing is also referred to as wholeness or oneness. Shifting into wholeness or oneness from polarity *shifts you to a state of higher consciousness. Wholeness or oneness is a higher state of consciousness than duality or polarity. And higher levels of consciousness can heal the lower levels.* In this state, the mind, body and soul come into harmonious vibrational alignment and the intelligent energy which permeates the body can "unblock" and flow with ease through you. In a state of wholeness or healthy flow, the body can do much to heal and restore itself.

There is little peace, and joy is all too fleeting when there is constant swinging between the poles. Give yourself a feeling of calm and relief from the spinning and worrying mind by embracing both sides of a situation. Look for until you find *both* the negatives and the positives of what is happening—for there are equal and opposite charges embedded in everything. An attitude of allowing or wholeness enables you to get off the swing for a little while. Allowing brings a feeling of peacefulness and is restful, restorative and revitalizing. Be alert to the moments when you are particularly caught up in polarity and judgment. *Try* to stop judging and labeling life. Try not to get caught up so much in "this is good" or "this is bad" and shift to simply "*this is.*" Adopt the view of "this is...*something*", "this is...*interesting*" or "this is ...*life*" instead.

Make a point of noticing when you are investing a lot of energy in being right or pointing out what is wrong, forcing or defending your position, trying to control others or the situation, seeing a given situation from only one perspective, or getting caught up in constant worrying. Ask yourself if you are enjoying this, or if this is upsetting or exhausting you by expending your energy this way. If the answer is the latter, give your mind and body a break by shifting to the perspective of allowance or wholeness. *Let go* of labeling and judgment as often as you can, allow the other perspective (which does not mean agreeing with it), thus adopting a whole instead of a one-sided perspective. There is peace and stillness in wholeness, or allowance. This level of consciousness permits you, for the time being, to step off the swing of life and be revitalized.

It is especially important to let go of judging yourself so harshly and your body. This is not only exhausting, it is destructive. *Self-worth is crucial to having a healthy body and a happy life* (more on self-worth in Chapter Five). Try to *just be* with things, and with yourself. Stop trying to *be perfect* (which is polarity and definitely not wholeness or oneness with *all* that you are) and just *perfectly be*. It is natural to evaluate or judge constantly (which usually means criticizing yourself) but you can cultivate a different habit with practice. Remember, choosing one side or pole (i.e., judgment) means resisting the other side or pole and resistance creates a block in the energy of things, including the energy of your body. Getting to wholeness/allowance by letting go of the habit of harshly judging who you are and your physical body may not be easy, but with enough conscious awareness and persistence, habits can be changed. Once you have achieved this frame of mind, the energy is unblocked and your body is able to flow in a natural and healthy way.

Try to be in the present moment. The mind has a propensity to dwell in the past or worry about the future. This habit of the mind facilitates the emotional swings, whereas keeping your focus or awareness on what is happening in the present moment lessens the swings and helps bring peace of mind. Life only happens in the present moment. If you forget to focus on the present moment, life will pass you by. Remember, you really only have the present moment to live!

Seek out the wisdom and solitude of nature to help you find wholeness and balance. Plant and animal life can give you energy. All of nature can give and receive without reservation for it functions from a perspective of wholeness which allows life's vital energy, *love,* to flow freely. (Love is the energy of higher consciousness or wholeness/oneness). We can learn a lot from animal and plant life for they truly know how to flow. We are not here to teach nature anything. *Nature is here to support and teach us.* There is no stupidity in nature — only wisdom.

Nature operates from heart wisdom (i.e., Source wisdom). Nature is free from judgment and polarity; the human mind is not, and that does lead to a lot of dumbness and stupidity. Nature is all about living life in the present moment. In Mother Nature's incredible presence, human beings can usually suspend judgment too and for the moment, be *fully present* and go with the flow of all of life (oneness). Silence (and I would add, nature) truly is "golden" for it transports you to a level of higher consciousness. It transports you to love and light.

Love is found in the synthesis of the positives and negatives of life

Just as life contains both ends of the continuum and every shade in between, so do *we*. Our very nature is both positive and negative charges. We are *all* things. Take every adjective that can describe human behavior that you can find in the dictionary — good, bad, honest, dishonest, passive, aggressive, kind, hurtful etc. Eventually, if we are honest with ourselves, we all exhibit each and every trait.

Not only is every situation composed of positive and negative charges — but *every thing is,* even you! Light itself is a combination of an equal amount of positively and negatively charged subatomic particles. Life is an equal balance of both positive and negative charges. You are a balance of both. Why does life aim for a balance between the positive and the negative charges? Why when your life is skewed to one pole does life move to bring you more of the other such that you are brought back to center, to equilibrium? The answer lies in the moment of equilibrium itself — which is the moment of perfect balance, the moment when polarity "collapses into itself" and the two poles fuse into one *whole*. Here, in a state of *wholeness*, in the absence of emotional swings, we arrive at a very special place in time. This place of wholeness, of perfect balance between positive and negative charges is *the place where pure love resides*. Pure love is a *synthesis* of polarity or life's opposites. Love is *not* found in the absence of negatives, but in the *allowance* of the negatives along with the positives. Pure or true love is without conditions. Pure love embraces both sides — it is wholeness. *Life keeps bringing you back to the middle, to equilibrium because it aims to bring you back to love. Life reminds us continuously that love is really what life is all about.* Love is allowing. Love is wholeness.

Consider the circumstance when someone does something great for you, and you feel you love them. However, when they do something you can't stand, you now feel you hate them. In this example, the first emotion was not true love. If you are caught on a swing from one extreme to the other, you are experiencing infatuation in that moment, not true love. Love does not leave you swinging. It is steady. It is stable. It is whole. It is the moment where you simply *know* you love the person, with all their so-called good or bad points — in fact *because of* their good and bad points — because that is the unique combination of ingredients which makes them, them. In the moment you feel love, you are moved, perhaps even to tears, but you are *literally moved*. That is, you have *transcended to a higher place.* You have left duality behind and moved to wholeness, to the place where love resides. *Pure love is a state of higher consciousness.*

This is love: to fly toward a secret sky, to cause a hundred veils to fall each moment. First, to let go of life. Finally, to take a step without feet.

Jalaluddin Rumi (1207-1273), poet, mystic

When you acknowledge the perfection or miracle of your life with all its positives and negatives, you find yourself experiencing pure or unconditional love for life. When you embrace both poles (allowance), the swings collapse and you are transported to a state of higher consciousness, a state of wholeness, or simply, love. Wholeness = Love = Consciousness. In the instant of the collapse, depending on the particular circumstances, you may suddenly feel *more alive* or even overwhelmed with the sense that you *just love life* or just love your mate, your pet, all of nature, or yourself! Pure or unconditional love is what pure white light is to the colors of the rainbow. It is not the absence of anything. It is the summation or sum total of it all. Your soul or spirit resides permanently in the moment of collapse of the two poles, which is the place of stillness, peace and wholeness, the place where love resides. This is also the place where all of the animal and plant life of the planet resides. *This is where the Source resides.*

Love is your eternal soul, your true nature and your physical body. Your flesh and blood is love (at a much lower vibratory level). You are love. Your soul is on a mission seeking growth, and it is seeking the highest feeling of love — which is the highest level of consciousness. Growth and love may seem like two different things, but upon closer examination, you can see that they are one and the same. Growth is the expansion of everything, or the All-That-Is. Love is the synthesis of everything, or All-That-Is. Growth = Love = Everything! Love is the force of consciousness. Love is the driving force of evolution and all of creation. There is no greater power. *Love is the Source.* Love = All-That-Is = Consciousness = Source = *You.*

Love builds. Love evolves. Love expands. And love creates. Love is the essence of every particle of matter which is at the core of every form of life imaginable. The essence of everything in the natural world is *the same — it is love.* This is why we are all *one* with each other and with *every* life form on the planet. You are on a journey of growth and evolution — which is the same as saying you are on a journey to the highest level of consciousness — which is the same as saying you are on a journey to the highest feeling of love.

The ultimate experience in life is love. The ultimate lesson is love. *At the core of every issue that happens in your life is a lesson in love* — love of the self (self-esteem), love of the other, love of all life. You need to connect to the love *within* first, in order to connect in love with others and the world around you. Connecting with love and compassion both within and without is essential to experiencing joy in life.

Your task is not to seek for love, but merely to seek and find all the barriers within yourself that you have built against it.

Jalaluddin Rumi (1207-1273), poet, mystic

If you want others to be happy, practice compassion. If you want to be happy, practice compassion.

The Dalai Lama (1935-), Buddhist spiritual leader of Tibet

You also need to connect and nurture the love within (i.e., honor your own worth) in order to heal your body. Finding your way back to wholeness, to self-love, is crucial to the experience of joy in life and good physical health — it restores balance to your entire being (to be discussed in Chapter Four).

The ultimate answer to any question in life is — what would love do? The main pathway to learning and navigating well through life is through the *heart*, not the mind. The heart does not learn by thinking. It learns by *experiencing*, by *feeling*. By learning to follow our inner guidance or heart's wisdom, we grow and the heart expands. With the heart's expansion, love expands, and the soul experiences a higher level of consciousness, a higher feeling of love. *Everything* that comes at you in life, every experience you are having, no matter how you feel about it, comes at you from a place of love, to teach you love, and returns to love. It comes at you as an opportunity for growth, which is an opportunity for you to experience or *feel* love in a new way. As a result, *you* expand. And when you expand, the All-That-Is expands through you.

If love is a synthesis of all feeling, in order for the soul to experience the highest feeling of love, it must experience every feeling. It must experience the All-That-Is. At the level of wholeness, there is no judgment, all manner of things are not bad or good, they just are. Having said that, most of us cannot conclude that acts of cruelty or violence "just are" and maintain a loving or allowing attitude towards them simply because they are part of the All-That-Is. This is because the force of all life, while passing no judgment, continuously tugs and pulls at all of life in an endless effort to reach higher and higher levels of consciousness (which is love). The direction of evolution is towards higher levels of love. Once having experienced the less evolved qualities, man can move forward to make more evolved choices and work from the loving qualities of higher consciousness. Mankind does not need to keep *recreating* and living from his lower, less evolved or unloving attributes — it is enough to *remember* that those less evolved aspects exist and move on. Move on to the higher qualities of the soul, to the qualities of consciousness.

Your soul is on a journey to the highest level of consciousness, to the highest feeling of love. You can facilitate this journey, and foster good physical health, by stopping your mind from levying harsh judgments against yourself and others. Respect yourself and your deepest feelings i.e., your heart's wisdom. You can also facilitate the journey of your soul by respecting and behaving compassionately towards others and all forms of life. See the dramas in your life for what they really are — learning and growth opportunities — life "loving you" into an expanded version of yourself. If you are caught up in drama and it is distressing you, aim to find the learning and move on.

Animal and plant life are here to support our journey

We live on a beautiful, unique planet with the widest variety of life imaginable. A miraculous explosion of life forms is all around us and awaits our discovery. The natural world provides, through its endless offerings of shape, color, texture, aroma, taste, sound, and endless events and situations, a vast resource to stimulate and inspire our journey of growth. Once again, we are not here to teach nature anything; nature is here to support and teach us. Nature flows first and foremost on a *feeling* level. All of nature provides energy, inspiration and contrast to ignite our senses, feelings, passions, imagination, creations, learning and growth. The vast expanse of nature supports humanity's expansion. Together, we are part of a much larger whole that we can only begin to imagine.

The entire natural world, especially animal life, provides the vital support we need to accomplish all that we came here to do. Animals contribute their energies to the overall energy and well-being of our planet in ways we are only beginning to understand. Also, animal life stimulates our feelings and thought processes, especially the feelings of joy and love. Experiencing animal life warms and softens our hearts. *It causes us to be less in our minds and more in our hearts.* Feelings are energy and we create from feelings first. Our experiences of animal life encourage us to create from a higher, more benevolent energy — heart wisdom. When we create from the energies of joy and love, we expand the higher qualities of the soul, which are all based in love.

We can look to animals as a source of wisdom and learn from them. *Feeling* is the natural language of the planet and animals are exquisitely in tune with their feelings. They are in tune with the wisdom of their hearts instinctually. Consequently, they know things about the planet — they sense danger, earthquakes, the presence of water, etc. Your pet understands you on the basis of your feelings reflected in your intonation. Their instincts/feelings allow them to be "one" with the planet. Animals reside in wholeness — beyond polarity. They respect the planet and each other. Yes, they kill for their own or their offspring's survival, but beyond that, they are benevolent. They take only what they need. Mankind cannot boast such an evolved state. We are not here to be (nor are we) superior to any other form of life. On the school of Earth, we are exposed to many life forms to *teach us* to be benevolent and compassionate towards all life. Animals are here to support what human beings are trying to accomplish — to grow and experience the higher qualities of the soul, and in turn *to expand those higher qualities to new heights*. Animals can help us learn patience, compassion, kindness and love. Any one with a pet can attest to those qualities in their pet. They know their pet feels and exhibits love. The presence of animals and their gentle souls teaches us to be benevolent to all life.

I have kept the following poem in a file since I was a teenager. It touched my heart in such a profound way and I thought I'll keep it, for someday I would have a place to put it. I had forgotten all about it until just recently, as I was writing this section of the book, memory of it popped into my head out of nowhere, out of the so-called void, and into my mind. And it occurred to me — this is the place for the poem that I have kept for decades because a part of me knew I would have a use for it some day.

Kinship

I am the voice of the voiceless;
Through me the dumb shall speak,
Till the deaf world's ear be made to hear
The wrongs of the wordless weak.

From street, from cage, and from kennel,
From stable and zoo, the wail
Of my tortured kin proclaims the sin
Of the mighty against the frail.

Oh, shame on the mother of mortals
Who have not stooped to teach
Of the sorrow that lies in dear, dumb eyes,
The sorrow that has no speech.

For the same force formed the sparrow
That fashioned man and king;
The God of the whole gave a spark of soul
To furred and to feathered thing.

And I am my brother's keeper,
And I will fight his fight,
And speak the word for beast and bird
Till the world shall set things right.

Ella Wheeler Wilcox (1850-1919), author and poet

All animal and plant life need our support. They are leaving the Earth at an alarming rate. Every form of life on the planet needs us to change our ways. We are in need of a quantum leap in our *empathic or feeling connection with life.* The solutions will come from the wisdom of the heart first. Thought and behaviors will flow from there to produce the changes we need. We need to look within. We search for answers—love, the meaning of life and the Source of it all—outside of us. What if we put more emphasis on seeking and welcoming life, love, and the Source *within* us? As a species, we are quite disconnected from our true feelings, the wisdom of our heart. The answers to our problematic ways will emerge more from heart wisdom and less from mind wisdom—meaning we need to look to what we know to be true on a *feeling* level first. Ideas and the how-to steps will follow from the heart or feeling wisdom (more on heart wisdom in Chapter Three). We look to others, to science, to "wise leaders" for answers which is all fine—but all too often we look for the answers outside of ourselves without listening to the wisdom within and following our own heart.

In summary, aim for benevolence and respect for all life

Universal intelligence embedded in each particle of life is always expanding. You are Source energy, higher consciousness, manifested as a human being—a walking, talking, feeling, thinking miracle! We are inextricably linked like a symphony conducted by a source of intelligence and love beyond our wildest imagination. All of life is inextricably linked in a symbiotic relationship of mind-boggling proportions that we will forever endeavor to understand. You are part of all life and the All-That-Is is part of you. Life is evolving—around you, through you, as you. From the subatomic perspective, all life is one, be it human, animal, plant or mineral. All life is sacred, vital, interconnected, and equal. You are a tiny piece of Mother Earth. The same elements that make up her body make up your body—predominantly water and minerals. All physical forms of life eventually die and its elements return to Earth to be reborn in the next physical form—the next walking, crawling, flying or swimming marvel of creation. Thus each life form sustains the next, be it a mineral, a tree, a lake, a bird, an animal, a person. All life is interdependent and when we treat *any* aspect of Mother Earth in a non-benevolent way, we harm ourselves because ultimately, *her body is our body. Treat your Mother well!*

We are all one at the particle level, and all particles are consciousness in a slower vibration. If human particles are ensouled, and every form of life is the same on the particle level, does that mean that animal life is ensouled also? You only have to look into the eyes of an animal or your pet to know this is true. It would follow that *all* offspring of the Mother are infused with a spark of life force or soul energy. Every form of life is ensouled — even plants and minerals. Even the Earth herself is ensouled! Wow! What does your mind think of that?!

For this moment in eternity, your soul picked to be, in part, in physical form on planet Earth (the larger aspect of it remains in the non-physical or realm of higher consciousness) with all its incredible physical beauty and diversity. Your physical self is on the leading edge of creation, and you from a non-physical or consciousness perspective will expand as a result of this experience. Each of us, each tiny, unique and vital spark of the whole of consciousness is ever learning, ever growing and ever expanding. Thus the Big Picture gets even bigger. All that happens to you along the journey of your life is part of your growth experience and as such contributes to the growth of it all. You will expand as a result of having experienced this life of yours with all of its ups and downs and as a result of whatever comes after it, after the death of your physical body. Your expansion is eternal as the energy that is *you* is eternal.

The soul knows only peace and love. Humanity's challenge in physical life is to remember or rediscover the truth the soul already knows, and take it to new heights. Actions on the Earth plane can only be benign if we allow ourselves to be guided by the wisdom of our hearts and the higher qualities of the soul. The well-being of you, humanity, and the planet depends on this.

There is more hunger for love and appreciation in this world than for bread.

Mother Teresa (1910-1997), nun, missionary, Nobel Prize for Peace, 1979

As you navigate through daily life, with every decision you are facing or choice you need to make, ask yourself first—what would love do?—including love for yourself, love for the other and love for other life forms. Let love be your guide. Remember these truths your soul already knows on a higher plane and try your best to draw from them when you are struggling on the Earth plane. As we rediscover our true nature and embrace the higher qualities of the soul, we can see more clearly the insanity of treating ourselves, our fellow man and all other life forms poorly. All life forms are striving to create a *good life*. *Start with loving yourself—mind, body and soul. It is only when you fill yourself up with love that you have any to give away to others, the animals and the planet.*

As we evolve, we are better able to embrace and further develop the higher qualities of the soul. The material world we experience is a product of our collective consciousness. The energy of our collective thoughts, attitudes and feelings surrounds and permeates us—it is as real as the air we breathe. Each one of the Earth's approximate seven billion people adds to this energetic atmosphere and is affected by it. Thoughts of violence or hatred contribute to wounding the planet and take it "off balance" energetically, which eventually manifests physically. Thoughts of loving kindness heal the planet, restore balance or wholeness and add to material abundance, globally. A better world starts with each individual releasing the lower qualities from their ego-based mind and holding more compassion in their heart. We are capable of making more evolved choices.

Could the poles humanity experiences soon change? That is, will we in our lifetime see significantly "less negative" negatives and "more highly evolved" positives in daily life on Earth? We can hope that mankind has now learned enough on his journey i.e., that collective consciousness has now evolved far enough that we do not require so much *actual experience* of the negative contrast to know the kind of world we would like to create going forward. It is enough to know about the negatives based on our collective history and memory as opposed to the situation where we continue to keep *recreating* the highly negative contrasts such as conditions of war, poverty and cruelty. Humanity's collective mission lies in the practice of love and compassion. Hold these hopes for the further evolution of mass consciousness in your heart—compassion and abundance for all, and the healing of the entire planet and natural world—and in so doing, you will contribute to the build up of these desired outcomes energetically. Thought eventually gives way to form. The greater the energy behind the thought, the faster the outcome materializes.

Lengthen your time spent in tranquil moments and in the quiet wisdom and stillness of nature. Love resides there. Also, in the course of daily life, remember to retreat to the place where love resides within— in your own heart. The love of Source within is found by entering the stillness or warmth within i.e., by being not doing, by calming your mind and by opening your heart to yourself and focusing on its love and warmth. Focus on this loving, warm feeling in your heart or solar plexus often, even if only for a few moments—breathe it in and imagine it spreading throughout your body. If you like, imagine this loving energy spreading out from you and blanketing the entire planet.

The love of Source within is also fostered by being with the ones you love. Your tri-part being wants you to spend time in the place of love or wholeness as often as you can because once there, the energy of love, which already permeates your body, is free to flow unblocked and can nurture and restore you, unfettered by the negative distractions and distortions of the mind. You can contribute energy to the uplifting of the planet by uplifting your own tri-part being. As you are restored and revitalized by the healing energy of love, you have more to give. As more people spend time in their heart, mass consciousness will shift and humanity will experience a quantum leap towards peace and well-being for all life. Expansion and growth is what life is all about. But it is also about our experiencing the evolution of love and the joy of living along the way. Life is all about reaching the higher, loving qualities of the soul, pulling them down from their heights to all life forms on Earth in the course of the daily life we create, so that we can pull all of life up!...And ever upward...

Chapter Three

MIND, BODY AND SOUL

A physical, mental, emotional and spiritual approach to wellness takes into consideration who-you-really-are — a tri-part being. Mind, body and soul — you are the *whole of it*. There are no true divisions. This chapter aims to give you a better understanding of each facet of *you*. From that understanding, you will come to know what changes are needed in your four great modes of experiencing life — physical, emotional, mental and spiritual — in order to bring your tri-part being back into harmony so that you can maximize your well-being in every way. When an aspect of you is unwell or in pain, your entire tri-part being is out of balance. To find your way back to well-being, you will need a return to wholeness and to a balanced approach to life. The maintenance of good health, or healing if you are unwell, comes from the power of the mind and the heart, linked with the power of the soul. (The subjects of health and healing are discussed further in Chapter Four.)

You are a tri-part being—mind, body and soul

Despite any physical problems you may have, your *life* is not about what your *body* is doing. But your *body* is all about what your *life* is doing! Your body is a *reflection of your state of being*. Your thoughts, feelings and outlook or approach to life are woven into the very fabric of your body. The health of your body is a reflection of the state of your mental, emotional and spiritual health. Your body is your soul or spirit made manifest i.e., consciousness slowed to a much lower vibratory level. You are consciousness, an aspect of which is presently focused on a physical or material life. You exist in this physical time-space reality, while retaining your higher non-physical perspective (the perspective of higher consciousness, the soul).

Your body is your means of *experiencing* the life your soul has conceived of and the world your mind has created. Your body is your vehicle—literally your consciousness or soul in *motion,* in physicality, in molecules vibrating. We forget how special the body is. You are not a physical being that has a temporary spirit—but a spirit that temporarily has a body. The body truly is the temple of the soul while you are in this lifetime of yours—a walking, talking, creating, growing, experiencing miracle! So honor your temple by taking good care of your body. However, in order to maintain good health or heal the body, you also need to heal your mind and find a balance within your tri-part being so that your soul's loving high energy can flow freely and nurture you. The power of higher consciousness can heal lower levels of consciousness. Or to put it another way, the power of the soul can heal the mind and the body, when there is a focus on returning to wholeness and a balanced approach to life.

You are a creator, a spark of the Source, which is presently focused on creating and experiencing the physicality of life. As a result, the consciousness which *you* are on a higher plane will expand, as will all of creation, as will the Source of it all. You are here on the leading edge of creation for the pure joy of creating, experiencing and expanding. All the elements of the physical world are at your disposal — as your teachers, your artistic inspiration, your clay and your smorgasbord of physical life! Your tri-part being is busy creating your day-to-day life: the soul *conceives,* the mind *creates,* the body *experiences.* Or, to put it a different way, the soul *chooses,* the mind *knows,* the body *acts.* And how do your emotions fit into this equation?

Feelings are generated by the soul and interpreted by the mind

Feelings serve to link together the three aspects of *you*. Feelings are generated by the soul. We are feeling beings, first and foremost. Your natural or *true* feelings are soul-based and are inherent. They originate from your soul and as such they are in alignment with your true nature and guide you to your highest good. Of course they come through the mind, or you would have no knowledge of them, but they are not *of* the mind. I say *true* feelings in order to distinguish them from the great volume of thoughts and emotion that the mind generates in response to your natural feelings. While your true feelings originate from the soul, they are interpreted and operated on by the mind. Your mind can interpret and "handle" your true feelings directly and effectively i.e., it can identify, express and resolve them as need be. Or, the mind can *mishandle* or *distort* your natural, inherent feelings i.e., fail to recognize them, misidentify them (cover one up with another) or pump them up — thereby *failing to resolve them* and instead producing a great deal of unwanted, unhealthy thoughts and subsequent emotion.

Your soul is operating from a higher perspective, the perspective of consciousness, your true nature. You might like to think of it as the older, wiser you. From the soul perspective, you know who-you-really-are; you know the value of who-you-really-are; and you know what you want to create, learn and experience during your life on the physical plane. Your true feelings form the basis of this knowledge from your soul. Your soul's guidance comes to you in the form of natural feelings in your body. They are a form of guidance from your wiser, non-physical or consciousness perspective as you navigate through physical life.

Your true feelings are cues which when followed keep you in alignment with the wisdom of your "higher self". The feelings in your body—you may know them as "gut feelings" or a "knowingness-of-the-heart"—alert you to the path of your highest good, which is the same as saying the path leading to your personal growth, expansion or the path of greatest love. A good gut feeling in your solar plexus or chest area informs you that you are acting in alignment with your core values, in alignment with the wiser perspective of the consciousness that is *you*. This action will produce energy which is high in vibration which will in turn leave you feeling good and energized. It follows that a bad gut or heart feeling tells you that you are proceeding in a way that is contrary to your values or qualities of your soul. This action will produce low or distorted energy and you will feel poorly or drained. This is a cue to you that you need to take action to resolve your feelings and realign yourself with the path of your highest good. I refer to your true feelings as "heart wisdom". (True feelings, i.e., heart's wisdom, are elaborated on later in this chapter. Chapter Five describes the true or natural feelings in detail and the steps to take to resolve them.)

I distinguish your *true* feelings, originating from your soul or higher consciousness, from thoughts and emotions generated by your mind because the land of emotion can be confusing. Being in a physical body means having a mind — and having a mind means having an ego. (The ego is discussed in greater detail later in this chapter.) The ego is fear-based and is prone to distorting our natural or true feelings, particularly fears. The ego operates under a false idea that we are not-as-good-as the other i.e., we are not equal. Being human means having this fear from very early on in our development. But to what degree we doubt we are equal depends upon the quality of love we received in childhood, what was modeled to us by our parents, and how much we work on, over the course of our life, admitting and resolving our fears and developing our self-esteem. Depending upon the strength of our self-esteem, or sense of self-worth, the fear-prone, ego-based mind is capable of resolving our doubts about our worth or *pumping them up* thereby *distorting* them.

The egoic mind tends to distort natural or true fears and produces *fear-based thoughts "masquerading" as true feelings* which we know as a sense of inferiority. Inferiority or inadequacy is a fear-based, distorted and painful emotion. It is generated by the mind, not the soul. As a psychological defense for the painful emotion of inferiority, the mind can generate a "cover up" emotion of superiority. This mind-based emotion of superiority can lead to further distorted emotion and consequent distorted behavior such as hatred or violence. Both a sense of inferiority and superiority are products of the mind. When we have such distorted emotions, we can face them and resolve them, or else get "stuck" in them. Getting stuck in them often results in our becoming convinced these distortions of the mind are true i.e., we really are inferior or superior. If we fail to resolve the distorted emotion, if the mind is allowed to go "unchecked", it will lead to a cascade of subsequent emotions and actions which will generate a great deal of toxic energy in the body — which says nothing of the negative impact it can have on the well-being of others.

We are all familiar with the experience of the mind seeming to have its own mind and it playing undesirable thoughts, such as self-deprecating ideas about one's body or abilities, or worst-case scenario worries, over and over like a tape recorder that we cannot seem to shut off. This in turn generates a stream of distorted, unresolved emotions which generate energy that can be quite destructive to your being, depending on the particular "tape of the day". For example, if you believe that you are incapable, ugly, stupid or inadequate in some other way, you will generate distorted emotion (i.e., fear which is not resolved in a healthy way, so it gets distorted and you get stuck in it) which leads to distorted energy in your body. Conversely, if you believe you are worthy—e.g., talented, beautiful, smart etc.—you will generate high vibratory, uplifting energy in your body. The stronger your beliefs, the more energy they generate and the stronger the impact will be on your body. "I am_____" are arguably the most powerful words in the English language. How does your mind complete that sentence? Over time, low vibratory or unhealthy emotion can burden your immune system and lead to *dis*-ease and disease.

Feelings inspire or prompt you to act

Whether generated by the soul or the mind, feeling is felt by the body and its purpose is to inspire or prompt *action*. The role of the body is to act and feel or experience (experiencing is a form of action) the physicality of life. Feelings are intended to encourage and direct action. Your emotions strongly influence what you ultimately create. They link your soul and mind to your physical body. Emotions are energy in motion, or *"e-motions"*, and they inspire more *motion!* And as energy is vibration, *emotions produce a vibration within you*. Different emotions produce different vibrations. Some are higher, feel better and are more energizing (e.g., laughter, love) than others. Some feel draining, sickening or even nauseating (e.g., chronic fear, put downs or hatred). This is what is meant by "good or bad vibes". You feel them. They can be sensed by others — hence the expressions, "You can feel the vibe from him/her." And, "You can feel the vibe in the room." And given the Cosmic Law of Attraction (that which is like unto itself is drawn) emotional vibrations will draw more and more of that *same* vibration to you. Over time, emotions create chronic vibrational patterns in your body. This is why it is essential to your health to pay attention if you are not resolving your feelings or are stuck in an undesirable or unhealthy "tape recording" of distorted emotion in your mind e.g., chronic worries or deprecating thoughts about yourself or others. If you have conscious awareness that you have become stuck, you can make a conscious effort to resolve it and get *unstuck!*

Your soul (in the form of your true feelings or heart's wisdom) and mind produce feelings for you to experience and act upon and thereby they influence your process of creating the life you came here to have. A feeling will inspire you to take action to bring about more of that feeling, if it is desirable. Or, an unwanted or bad feeling will prompt you to take action in order to reduce it. This will result in you making a change and thus a different feeling will be generated — which in turn will inspire another action and another feeling and on it goes.

Pain and illness is a powerful prompt for action

All feelings prompt you to take some sort of action. Your action results in something changing in your life. Something new is then created — and change is what life is all about. The more discomforting or painful your feelings are, the quicker you will likely act on them. Physical pain gets our attention quickly. Pain performs a self-protective function. If you put your hand on something hot which will burn you, the pain you feel will prompt you instantly to take your hand off of it. If you are injured in some way, or if the source of your pain is unknown, we usually seek medical attention. It may well be that the change that is needed is something pertaining to a physical problem. However, it is also quite possible that the action that is being prompted by the painful feeling in your body *may have nothing to do with your physical health directly but most certainly has everything to do with your well-being in life.*

Of course, if you are having pain, your physical body is involved, and you need to take some form of action to soothe or repair it. But the painful feeling may have something more to do with an under-lying problem, something that needs your attention *other than* your physical health. For example, that pain in your lower abdomen may be indicative of an inflammatory or disease process, which may now be a real physical problem, but it may have begun and is being per-petuated because you are in a relationship which is in fact not good for you. That pain in your lower back could have started as a result of the fact that you worry too much and need to take steps to give yourself a greater feeling of security or support. Your shoulder pain may be the result of the fact that you are overburdening yourself emotionally by trying too hard to please everyone around you.

Your consciousness is all about valuing who you are i.e., self-worth and love. These high qualities of the soul have high vibrations. (Love is the highest vibration.) Your soul is all about high, healthy vibra-tion. If you are not on the path of your self-worth, of your true feel-ings, of your core values, you will manifest low or unhealthy energy which means your tri-part being becomes *out of vibrational alignment* and body, mind and spirit cannot function harmoniously. As a result, you will not feel good in your body and you will not feel happy in your life. You will need to act to resolve your feelings and realign your actions to be consistent with your core values and self-worth. There are no true divisions between your spirit, your thoughts, your emotions and your body. Your physical body is a reflection of the state of health and harmony of *all* aspects of you. And your body will alert you if there is disharmony. *An unwanted feeling in your body, illness, or pain is a consequence of your thoughts, emotions or actions being out of alignment or balance with your true nature (spirit or soul) – which is love.* When you are out of vibrational alignment, you are in a state of resistance. Your being's energy is discordant or blocked and you do not flow with ease with life. A state of resistance means you are not in allowance, wholeness or flow (in an energy sense), which also means you are not on the path of your highest good, and that does not feel good to your body.

If your thoughts are devaluing of yourself or others, if you are not treating your body with love and respect, if your actions are not in alignment with the higher qualities of your soul — then *you,* the tri-part being that you are, is out of balance or in a state of disharmony. This disharmony results in a discordant or unhealthy vibration between mind, body and soul, which in turn produces unwanted or bad feelings in your body. Should the discordant energy be chronic, it may eventually result in the body's systems malfunctioning or breaking down, producing physical pain or illness.

Pain or illness is not "sent by" your soul because you are failing to "heed or obey it". There is *no* process whereby higher consciousness punishes lower consciousness — not between Source and you and not between your soul and the rest of you — if you do not "do what the higher power wants". Your soul, which is an aspect of Source, is love. It is all about higher or evolved qualities. Higher power, i.e., higher consciousness, is not about control, revenge, righteousness, rage, all of which are lower or less evolved qualities. Your body's experience of pain is a consequence of your tri-part being's lack of vibrational alignment, and being out of balance energetically simply does not feel good. (That being said, the mind cannot fully know the goals *you* had for yourself in this lifetime. It may be that on a higher plane, *you* have goals which involve illness or a physical impediment in this lifetime. Nevertheless, maintaining a balance in your tri-part being may still help you in that you will experience healing, although *healing* does not necessarily mean *curing*. See Chapter Four.)

Your body knows what is best for you. However, being of the Earth plane, being physical matter, your physical body gets bogged down by unhealthy energy in all of its many forms—such as poor quality food, pollutants, lack of exercise, chronic worrying, stressful situations etc. It is sometimes difficult to pick up your body's signals clearly, especially if you have been out of balance for a long time. You may have become very out of touch with your body. In time, chronic, unhealthy patterns may become "hardened" in place (or habitual) and you may not fully realize how unhealthy your body has become, or how good you *could* feel. You may have learned to just put up with or accept that your body feels badly. It has become the "new norm". Unlike your soul, your body knows bad feelings. It knows chronic discomfort or pain.

Your mind, also being of the Earth plane, knows pain. Plus your mind can generate its own low or painful energy in the form of a great deal of unwanted, unhealthy or distorted emotion which downloads unhealthy energy into your body. Discomfort or pain felt in the body prompts you to take action to alleviate the pain and redirect yourself to the path of your highest good. The required action may not just be about doing, it may also be about *thinking*. That is, *your body* may be prompting you to redirect your *acts or habits of thinking*. Your body may be trying to bring your attention to a stream of reoccurring, unwanted thoughts and resulting unhealthy emotions that may be counter to your best interests e.g., thoughts that devalue yourself and erode your self-worth. Thoughts which generate or draw to you unhealthy or low-frequency energy vibrations (e.g., self-deprecation, chronic fears, judgment, violence, rage) drain or distort the healthy energy reserves of your body. Thoughts which generate or draw to you high-frequency vibrations (e.g., generosity, joy, playfulness, creativity, compassion) augment emotional and physical health.

If you are caught up in unhealthy mental and emotional habits, if you are unable to decipher the body's message to act, or if you have an awareness of what action you need to take for your highest good but you are not taking it, you will likely find that your level of physical discomfort will gradually increase over time while your experience of happiness and general well-being decreases. Chronic pain or other physical symptoms may diminish for a while before returning even stronger than before. Or, pain may materialize in some place new in the body. Over time, this may result in reoccurring pain or cycles of pain. It may also result in the development of a disease.

 The part can never be well unless the whole is well.

Plato (427-347 BC), philosopher

The good news is if you are not conscious of needing to resolve your feelings or redirect your thoughts and/or actions, the cues in the form of unwanted feelings in your body will get stronger until your body has your attention! And if you feel the call to action via uncomfortable feelings or pain, but do not know what your body is trying to tell you, do not worry. You cannot go wrong by focusing your efforts on tuning into your true feelings (i.e., heart's wisdom) and following their guidance — which is the same as saying following the path your self-worth dictates. You have already taken some steps in the direction of self-love. You are looking for new strategies for achieving well-being and to facilitate the health of your tri-part being or you would not have bought this book.

The feeling prompt may be mild — time for a change, something could be better. Or in the case of pain, it is a strong message that some form of change or action is urgently needed to bring you back into alignment with who-you-really-are, love. The challenge is for you to learn what your body is trying to tell you and take the action that is truly in your best interest. Not always easy to do. Let self-worth or self-love be your guide. You may be thinking that this sounds "selfish" and that such selfishness would not be good for those around you. I would describe it as "self-full" and ask you — how can you feed a starving man if your own fridge is empty? The same goes for love — you cannot give what you do not have.

Heart wisdom

Your true or natural feelings are your guidance system. Your true feelings are wisdom or messages in the form of energy from the non-physical or consciousness aspect of you to your physical self. Feelings are the language of the soul. Feelings are the universal language. They come directly from your soul into your physical body. In fact, your mind is the last of your three-part-self to know your true feelings! Your true feelings flow from your soul to your body to your mind. Of course this all happens so lightening fast, you are not aware of these steps. It happens before you *know it*, literally! You just know that you feel something. True feelings are not *based* in the mind. (As stated, they must come through the mind, in order for you to know them, but they are not *of* the mind.) Your mind *may or may not* be guiding you in the direction of your highest good, in the direction of vibrational align-ment with your true nature, because the mind is prone to distorting or mishandling your natural feelings. Your mind does not fully know the

Big Picture of *you*. However, your soul *always* guides you in the direction of your highest good.

True or natural feeling, I call it heart wisdom, is your ever-present, built-in-from-birth guidance system. Heart wisdom is the bridge between the non-physical you and your physical body. True feelings are the wisdom of your soul in action through your body. They are inherent. You are never without your guidance system — the wisdom of the "older", "higher-reaching" perspective of the center-of-consciousness that you are. The wisdom of your soul is always present in you. It is as real and as here-and-now as the real feelings in your heart or gut. This wisdom, in the form of your natural feelings, will let you know if your thoughts and actions are in harmony with who-you-really-are. Unlike your mind, your soul *always* knows what is best for you and will *always* direct you to your highest good because your soul *never* doubts your worth. Unlike your mind, your non-physical soul cannot get "bogged down" or confused by the contrasts and discord of physical life (and unlike the mind, it does not have an ego which can create all kinds of trouble for you!) Consciousness, or the soul, is far-reaching and comes from the perspective of love. When you feel good in your heart, you know that your tri-part being — mind, body and soul — are balanced, are in alignment. You are not in a state of resistance and your energy is now free to flow with ease with life. Heart Wisdom = Your True or Natural Feelings = Consciousness or Awareness = Soul = Self-Worth = Wholeness = Feeling Good. Wow!

Instinct and inspiration come from the wisdom of the heart

Heart wisdom, the wisdom of consciousness (or the soul) is the same wisdom which, in the animal world, is referred to as instinct.

Animals follow their inner feelings and instinctively trust their exquisite ability to sense the feeling of the moment as a guide to their actions and ultimate survival. In the moment where survival is determined, feeling, not thinking prevails. Your own instincts are an example of the ever-present connection between your non-physical and physical aspects. Instinct is not mental. It is spiritual-physical. It is a gut feeling or an absolute knowingness in the heart. The mind generates a lot of "noise" that can get in the way. (I.e., the mind starts to question things because that is its job, or starts to distort your feelings because it operates with a fear-based ego.) Instinct bypasses the mind and in so doing, the message remains crystal clear and is therefore acted on right away. Literally, when you follow your instincts, you act without thinking about it. An example is the situation where you are about to step off the sidewalk and on to the street when you suddenly hesitate, just before a car goes speeding by that would have hit you if you had not hesitated. You *felt* the danger, before you saw the car. Your action, in this case the hesitation, was instinctual.

Animals operate from this spiritual-physical connection all the time. They act the moment they feel danger. They do not stop to question this feeling (i.e. to think about it). They act on it. Survival depends on it. Instinct is often passed off as a "lower" form of intellect when actually it is higher, so much so that it is of the spirit, not of the mind. It is no lowly form of intellect, for example, that allows animals to navigate the globe or a school of fish to move as one.

Creative ideas, epiphanies and inventions emerge from heart wisdom, from the wisdom of the qualities of the soul. Moments of genius and great inspiration come from a loftier place, a place which transcends intellect. Inspirations are gifts from the soul, passing through to awareness through a quieted mind. They are not the result of thinking and thinking. In fact they happen when you *stop* thinking — when you

get *out of your mind* and into your heart! The order of inspired creation is true feeling (consciousness or soul) first, then thought and ideas
flow from there. Not the other way around. Creation flows from the
top down, from higher vibration (soul) to lower vibration (mind and
matter).

The wisdom that is always available to us through our true feelings is essential in making the best decisions for maximizing happiness
and well-being in life. Your true feelings will inspire you to take the
action that honors and develops your self-worth. When you are not
engaging in action that is in alignment with your highest good (which
is always the path of self-love and personal growth), your body will
alert you by producing a feeling of discomfort, a discordant vibration,
often in your gut. It has been said that the heart of one's emotions lives
in the belly. This is a main reason why digestive problems, stomach
aches and irritable bowel syndrome are such common problems during times of stress. Such times are often times when you are being chal-
lenged to find your true feelings and to keep your thoughts and actions
in alignment with them.

Finding your heart's wisdom

You may be wondering—is there a method or some guidelines you
can use to help you more readily identify your true feelings? Because
sometimes that's easy and sometimes it's not. The answer is yes, and
detailed guidelines are provided in Chapter Five. There are five true
or natural feelings which are inherent and essential. They are love,
anger, fear, hurt and guilt. These five share a common foundation—
love is in the core of all five of these fundamental feelings. You may
be wondering how a feeling like anger can be produced from the guidance coming from your soul, which is all about love and your highest

values. The answer is that your true feelings, whether they are anger (i.e., a feeling of something being unfair to you), hurt (i.e., a feeling of being devalued), fear (i.e., fear for your safety), love (including caring and happiness) or guilt (i.e., having gone against your own values) — *are all variations of love – love for the self and for the other. Love is at the core of your five inherent or natural feelings, just as love is at the core of you.* All five feelings stem from love and inspire action that is in alignment with your self-worth or your highest good. Anger and fear, feelings that are typically referred to as "negative", are *not negative at all* if they prompt you to act in alignment with your self-worth and your core values.

Love is fundamental to both the processes of following your true feelings, and the acknowledgement of the feelings of the other and their equal rights to have their own true feelings. *Self-worth or self-esteem grows when you "own" your true feelings – which means identifying, speaking if need be, and following or acting on them, thereby resolving them.* Love prevails and grows — depending upon how you handle your feelings and those of anyone else involved in a given situation. The path of self-esteem development is based on *democratic principles of equal rights:* the rights of each individual to have their own feelings, the acknowledgement that each person's feelings are of equal value (i.e., each person's feelings are *right*, for *them)* and the negotiation of compromises which are fair to the feelings of all parties involved which resolves the feelings. When you own, follow and resolve your true feelings in true democratic fashion, the principles and values of the higher qualities of the soul are upheld and strengthened — love prevails and grows.

When you follow your true or natural feelings, the wisdom of your heart, love expands. Not only does your self-love grow, but depending on the situation, you provide a model, a source of inspiration for the other party (which may be a loved-one such as a family member, your partner, or your developing child) to grow their self-worth by identifying and following their true feelings too. The question I am asked most frequently as a psychologist is how to grow or bolster the self-worth (i.e. self-esteem). The answer is...identify, follow, and resolve your true feelings.

"Owning" your true feelings or heart's wisdom is essential for good health and happiness. It is one of the most important ingredients in the achievement of overall well-being. After over two decades of operating a clinical psychology practice, I am convinced that at the core of every presenting issue, without exception, *especially* those causing considerable discord, unhappiness or stress, is a self-worth or personal growth theme. Embedded in every problematic issue is an opportunity to grow your self-worth, an opportunity to further clarify and pursue your values, an opportunity to find your way back to the qualities of the soul, to love. Look for the lesson. Get the learning and growth and honor your self-worth. Self-worth is crucial to achieving optimal health and joy in living. Modeling self-worth to others is a great way to shine your light on the planet. There is no one who cannot follow your example and learn to value themselves.

Your greatest power is your self-worth. *Self-worth means feeling equal, not inferior or superior. When you are certain of your value, secure in your own worth, it is easy to be humble and certain of the worth of others. Then you can truly lift them up, and lift all of life up to the higher reaches of love.* Love is truly what life is all about. There is no greater power. Love is what *you* are all about literally, love in slower vibration, consciousness on an eternal journey to higher and higher experiences of love.

Only when your thoughts, feelings and actions are in alignment with your true nature, will you find well-being and happiness. You can find your way back to vibrational alignment — to harmony, wholeness, and the flow of life — by following the guidance of your true feelings which are always there for you to discover and act on. No one can be truly happy unless they are true to how they truly feel!

Consciousness, your true nature, connects to your body and mind via your true feelings. Your soul has all the patience imaginable and all the time imaginable—beyond what is imaginable, actually—for you to grow, for you to expand in love. Your feelings will keep prompting or cueing you, over and over, time and time again, to put you on the path of growth, the path of mind-body-spirit alignment, the path of love.

Heart wisdom is embedded deep within the core of your being and guides you to a path or course of action which is not only consistent with nurturing and valuing yourself but is also benevolent to all life around you. Heart wisdom is the answer to the question: What would self-love/love do? Think of this wisdom as emerging from the deep still waters of a lake (your true, persistent feelings) rather than from the chaotic motion of the waves on the surface (fleeting thoughts or distortions from your mind—whims or a passing mood) which change with the wind. Heart wisdom is accessed through the process of asking: What do you know in your heart of hearts to be true? What is in the highest good? What would love do? The answer will come in the form of a deep feeling—a good or warm feeling in your gut, solar plexus or heart, or a strong, unwavering inner *knowing*. Heart wisdom is that which you know "in every fiber of your being."

If you find your self at an impasse and you are wondering which direction is in your highest good to take or what option is congruent with the higher qualities of your true nature, you may wish to try the following exercise. Generate a few options, and then try to narrow the field down to just a couple. Do this exercise alone and calm your mind and body down so that you are in a relaxed state. This is a *feeling* exercise so try to "stay out of your mind" (!) and sense how you feel deep within you. Imagine you have chosen option "A". Now "pick this option up" in your imagination and "place it" squarely on your solar plexus or heart area — literally "try it on for size". Ask your body if this option is in the highest good. And wait quietly. See how you feel inside. Do you feel good, or warm, in your solar plexus, gut or heart? (You will learn in time where exactly you tend to feel your feelings best. It is likely in this general area of your body; however, some people may feel their deep feelings more in their back, neck or head areas.) Now try option "B" on for size and see how you feel. Be patient. You may need to try this exercise a few times or again the following day before you are sure of which option *feels* right to proceed with. (At worst, you may choose the wrong option. But you will soon know it is the wrong option because you will not *feel* good about it and can hopefully change course readily.) We can *feel* our way when we do not *know* the way.

The world needs more heart wisdom

We sometimes fail to listen to the heart, especially in this day and age where the mind tends to reign supreme. Too often, we are all about the "neck up". We tend to get caught up too much in the mind which wanders often into ego-based thoughts of inferiority, superiority, lack and greed — the mind truly is a product of duality which has great pros and cons. When the mind dominates, when we have had no quiet time to calm the mind and "check in" with our heart, when we forget our worth and forget to nurture the spirit, when our predominant feeling in the gut or heart is one of feeling bad — the tri-part being that you are will become out of balance. And then something has got to give — mind, body or spirit. You are then vulnerable to anxiety, depression, illness or an existential crisis. It is possible to get so lost in the ego and fear-based fantasies of the mind that we forget who-we-really are and life becomes meaningless, difficult or frustrating, joyless or worse. But the guidance of the heart and soul is always there for you to discover and bring you back into harmony. Love is always within you. Tune into it and nurture it. For love is what you-really-are.

The wisdom of our deepest, innermost feelings, our heart, always produces the best course of action for our well-being because at our core the only energy is love. Heart wisdom is the wisdom of higher consciousness; it is wisdom based in love. This wisdom always results in a benign course of action. Simply put, we need more heart wisdom in this world and less head wisdom (which may or may not be truly wise). A key factor to living a life of joy and well-being is to be more in the heart and less in the head. Look within, connect to your deepest feelings and intuitions, feel and listen to the wisdom of your heart. You may not always be able to hear your heart wisdom but it is ever-present in the quiet stillness within and you can learn to be a better listener! Your true feelings will guide you to love yourself and others more.

The answers to our strivings for peace and joy lie in the inner stillness and love which resides in the heart. All of humanity, the animals and the entire planet would benefit from man listening and following his heart wisdom. Solutions to our shared global problems including violence, war, hunger, pollution, disease, and the loss of animal and plant species will emerge if heart wisdom were to guide our decision-making. So too will the solutions to your life problems gradually emerge from being first and foremost in tune with your heart—the core of which is your self-worth, which inspires ideas and a course of action to maximize your own well-being. When you maximize self-love, your cup will overflow and you will have more love to extend to life all around you.

The mind

Arguably, nothing in the natural world comes close to matching the marvel of the mind. We acquire our knowledge of the world around us through our senses. We are lost in the world of our five senses, indeed the mind knows of no other reality. Although we may be in the habit of thinking that it is our eyes or ears, for example, that actually do the sensing, they do not. They are just the carriers of the vibrations coming from the outside world which are then presented to the mind for examination and interpretation. The brain slows life down—*it literally slows the vibrations of life down*—and encodes them electrically in a way that allows us to understand our surroundings. (On the way to our physical manifestation, first the soul slows the speed of vibration of Source energy, thereby transforming it. Our mind further reduces the rate of vibration of the life surrounding us so that we can physically process it and understand it. Wow!) All that we see, hear, taste, smell and sense is a result of the electrical activity of the mind.

The mind is curious and seeks to discover things. We are problem-solvers. We are creators. The mind aids in the process of creation by always wanting to know—how, why, what, where, who. The mind is a strong driving force in the creation and expansion of the All-That-Is. Life on planet Earth means having a mind. We cannot very well live without it, but all too often, we cannot live very well with it!

I have had more trouble with myself than with any other man I've met.

Dwight Moody (1837-1899), clergyman

The conscious mind doesn't know how to flow

The mind is a powerful creator. It is capable of creating so much that is good, and also so much which is not good. It is a product of duality. It operates from the perspective of the time-space reality of the Earth plane and as such is affected by the "rules of the road" here, including external societal influences which are full of contrasts and high and low (healthy and unhealthy) energies, and the internal construct, the ego (which is fear-based). The mind's activity works to interpret your true or natural feelings which are soul-based. It interprets them, thereby generating a host of thoughts about them, which in turn creates more emotion and may "pump up" the natural feelings. This mind-based emotion may be in alignment with your true feelings and the mind may eventually lead you to own (admit) and resolve your feelings. Or, this mind-based emotion can be a distortion of your natural feelings and then you believe and act upon these distortions or exaggerations. Either way — your mind interprets or operates on your true feelings, and the resulting cascade of thoughts and emotions (which are *energy-in-motion*) that the mind produces, impact the body. Your body experiences and is affected by the *energy* of your thoughts and feelings. The mind and body are *inseparable*. There are no true divisions between the aspects of your tri-part being. What the mind focuses on grows *substantially* i.e., thoughts give way to *substance* or matter. Your thoughts influence the *matter* that you are, biochemically — including immune, hormonal and inflammatory processes. This is why it is so important to pay attention to what you think about, and it explains the origin of the expressions, "You get what you think about." And, "What you focus on grows."

Also, the mind tends toward dwelling in the past (which no longer exists) or thinking about the future (which does not exist yet) as opposed to staying focused on *present* time, on what is happening now — the *only* moment where we are truly living!

Most people treat the present moment as if it were an obstacle that they need to overcome. Since the present moment is life itself, it is an insane way to live.

Eckhart Tolle (1948-), author

Thoughts of the past and future may be pleasant, which will generate positive emotion and positive energy (high vibrations) in the body. Unfortunately, the mind is prone to fear-based thinking—a habit which tends to worsen with age. This is because habits get more firmly entrenched over time and the closer to mortality we get, the more we have learned to worry and the longer we have had to practice. The mind frequently spends time brooding over what has happened that it considers problematic. And it is fond of projecting itself into the future where it imagines something to worry about. This will generate a great deal of unwanted, low-energy or distorted thoughts and emotions which will impact the body in a poor way.

Unwanted or low-energy natural feelings are not a problem for the body in and of themselves. In fact, they are a very important form of guidance, as are your high energy feelings of caring and love. All of your natural feelings, including anger, hurt and fear, act as guidance signaling you to take action and resolve them—or pursue more of it, in the case of your natural feelings of love and caring. However, unwanted or low energy feelings are a problem if you do not act upon them and instead find yourself dwelling or ruminating on them, which frequently results in the mind's pumping them up and distorting them. In other words, whatever you concentrate or focus on grows. Literally, the *energy* of it *expands* or magnifies. Your body is exposed to a steady "diet" of the mind's thoughts and emotions that will influence your overall energy level, health and well-being more than you realize. *Your thoughts and feelings translate into energy in your body as surely as the food or drugs that you ingest.*

The energy of the emotion you feel in your body signals you to *do* something. It is prompting you to take action to identify your true feelings (i.e., hurt, anger, fear, love and guilt—see Chapter Five for details) if they are not yet obvious to you (which is the case surprisingly often) and follow or act in accordance with them. This eases or resolves them and restores a harmonious feeling or healthy vibration in the body and restores the balance of your body's biochemistry.

If you find yourself stuck in a "tape recording" of the mind which is not good for you and/or devaluing to you in some way (e.g., stewing on undesirable events of the past, telling yourself repeatedly that you are unworthy, or dwelling on the what-ifs of the future), these thoughts and emotions translate at the physical level into a continuous stream of unhealthy energy and leave you in a disharmonious or unbalanced state, energetically speaking. This places a mounting burden on your body that it must work hard to try to overcome.

In short, the conscious mind tends to focus on undesirable events of the past, or fears of future and other negative "tapes" such as inadequacy fears. Unlike your soul, the conscious mind does not know how to *flow* with life. Again, this is why it is so important to *identify, listen and act* on your true or natural feelings, the wisdom and guidance from the older, wiser *you,* and restore the flow of healthy energy through your body. Your heart and soul know how to flow!

An important point to remember is that the habits of the mind — worrying about past and future and playing deprecating tapes over and over — are just that, habits. Habits are learned and can be unlearned. That is, with some practice and vigilance you can break unwanted habits and *change your mind!*

Change your mind or learn to "*re*-mind" yourself

Do not underestimate the powerful role the mind plays in both creating and alleviating the physical problems of the body. Do not underestimate the force! The mind is capable of bringing a great deal of pleasure or pain to your physical experiences. The mind is truly a powerful creator—fortunately, so are *you*! You just need to remind it that it is only one of the incredible and powerful aspects of the truly powerful tri-part being that you-really-are and teach it some new habits. Your physical body has a tremendous capacity to heal itself if left to its own devices. It engages in healing and restorative processes all the time—cuts heal, bones mend. The body is endowed with the wisdom of the consciousness that *you* are and as such, it has amazing capacities to heal itself that the world's best scientific minds cannot fully explain, let alone duplicate. The problems for the body arise as it is impacted upon by the negative byproducts of human activity, including the unhealthy habits of the mind. The physical and spiritual aspects of your being know how to flow. The mental aspect does not. In its efforts to clarify "this is this" and "that is that", to categorize and control life, and in succumbing to the habits of worrying and devaluing, the conscious mind slows or clogs the energy flow.

How do you work at *changing your mind*? There is so much you can do. Become more conscious of the things that you say to yourself out of habit or early conditioning. Let go of perfectionism, judgment and other negative or self-deprecating tapes. Stop thinking and talking about what you *do not* want. Keep your focus as best as you can on what you *do want*. Come back to the middle i.e., the attitude of allowing and wholeness (love), as often as you can. Keep your focus on honoring your self-worth and your values. Listen to your heart's wisdom. Pay more attention to what your body would like you to know and less to what the mind thinks it knows! Value your intuition. Focus on the qualities of higher consciousness e.g., loving relationships, fun, play, and creative pursuits. Remind yourself frequently to keep your conscious awareness on the present moment. Take a break from the mind by calming it through meditation and spending quiet time in the healing powers of nature. Wow! Focus on all that you *can* do. Your mind is not in total charge of you, despite its rather convincing rhetoric telling you that is. You have a say in the matter, even in the grey matter! The mind needs a push now and then towards growth and expansion.

You can work at the process of stemming the flow of unhealthy or distorted emotions from the mind into your body with persistence. I say work at it because we cannot be on top of our thought processes all the time. The mind likes what it is used to and will slip back into the familiar nature of old patterns. You may not be conscious of them in the moment because the conditioning returns with autopilot ease. You will need to be vigilant in your watch and observe your mind in order to break free from old, previously conditioned tapes and curtail the development of new undesirable ones. This may sound like too much work. Your mind may try to convince you that you cannot change it as it likes to be in charge. But with conscious awareness of conditioning you *can* shift out of it in short order and start to feel better. You *can* learn to identify and face your true feelings and resolve them. You *can* always give yourself more moments of peace of mind, calmness and joy. You *can* always take your focus off the past and future and bring it back to the present. The pay-off is a better quality of life. You cannot help but feel better when you do this because your tri-part being will move closer to alignment, to harmonious vibration, to the restoration of balance.

Positive thinking is great. However, positive feeling is even better (strong emotion associated with a given thought, magnifies the energy of that thought). If you focus on them, your thoughts give way to emotions which are very powerful. Your emotions are a powerful point of attraction. (The Cosmic or Universal Law of Attraction is summarized in the well-known expressions, "You get back what you give out."

And, "What you focus on grows.") Positive feelings (which are soon generated by putting your mind's focus on the love you have for yourself, others, and to the things you are appreciative of and enthusiastic about in your life) are the best possible gift you can give to yourself and the planet. When you are able to bring yourself back to such positive and loving feelings, you unblock or lighten your own energy. Then, not only do you feel good, you add lightness to the world around you. Remember, if you do not take charge of the mind, the mind can and will take charge of you, and you may not like the outcome.

The Ego

There is an aspect of the mind referred to as ego. Ego is "I" — our sense of self. It is our sense that we are separate, that we are an individual. Ego performs the functions of the mind which include judgment, reality-testing, defense, synthesis of information, memory, logic and abstract thinking. The concept of "I" or ego is abstract. There is no cellular matter you can point to that defines the ego. Nevertheless, a sense of "I "or ego exists. The ego allows us to organize our thoughts and make sense of the world. We all have an ego. We need an ego to function as an individual. Also, the ego keeps us believing that we are each an *individual*, functioning. But "I" is a *false* self for we are not truly separate. (Recall from Chapter One — there are no "empty spaces" or "gaps". All is Source energy and all is one.)

From the Big Picture perspective, "I" is a misperception of who-you-really-are. "I" is an *illusory* sense of identity. It lives on *i*-dentification and separation. Ego is the product of the individual mind. It is the product of being born into an individual body. It is the product of being in this time-space reality, of life with duality, of the illusion of a life separate from Source. Ego is the result of forgetting we are all one, there is no "other", and everything is really an extension of Source. Living in the illusion of individuation, we forget that we really have nothing to fear. Again, a shift to the Big Picture perspective temporarily shifts everything and fears can then dissipate. But as long as we are in physical form, we have an ego and it results in a great deal of fear-based thinking. We fear lack, we fear inferiority, and we fear "the other". In the absence of love, there is *fear*, not evil. There is no source of evil in higher consciousness which is also the source of your true feelings. However, on Earth, a great deal of evil is committed out of human fear. The mind's distorted fears are at the core of such emotions as rage, inferiority fears and superiority. Fear is at the root of such behaviors as controlling, bullying and violence – which result in evil doings.

The fear-based ego "resides" almost exclusively in the past or the future. It is the voice in the head which is constantly making comparisons and complaining. It has a mindset of *lack* and worries about " getting mine before you get yours". It *wants* all the time. It often has conflicting wants. Ego might not even know what it wants, but it knows it does not want *what is.* It does not want *the present moment.* Restlessness, boredom, dissatisfaction and anxiety are the result of unfulfilled wanting. The ego identifies with having, but is only satisfied with what it has for a short period of time, and then it wants something else.

In the core of the ego is a deep-seated dissatisfaction, of incompleteness, of not enough. These are the emotional "seeds" which can grow into significant inadequacy or inferiority feelings. The ego is the voice in the head that says – I do not have enough yet – which really means – *I am not enough yet.* Depending upon one's life experiences, the ego compares and declares – I am inferior or not as good as. Or, the ego tries to hide its fear of inferiority by declaring – the other is inferior, I am superior. But the ego is not comforted by that belief for long. Very soon, it generates once again a feeling of a lack of value or a lack of self-worth and becomes preoccupied all over again with — I do not have enough yet, I am not enough yet, I need more. Before we know it, we can get caught in a vicious circle. Unless we wake up to this, we can spend our entire life enslaved by the never-satisfied ego in the form of a sleepwalking or autopilot haze of the "false self". The false self is the state in which we continue to criticize and devalue ourselves and critique or even hate the other. Sounds insane doesn't it? It is! This is insane thinking (tremendously distorted thoughts and emotions). Such fear-based thinking results in our missing out on the wondrous beauty of who-we-really-are and who-the-other-really-is, and the magnificence and abundance that life all around us offers. Although there is no true devil or hell, the ego can create an internal state of mind as close to hell as one will ever get.

If you want to reach a state of bliss, then go beyond your ego and the internal dialogue. Make a decision to relinquish the need to control, the need to be approved, and the need to judge. Those are the three things the ego is doing all the time. It's very important to be aware of them every time they come up.

Deepak Chopra (1947-), physician and author

This fear-based aspect of the mind wants control over your life and is convinced that control is possible. It says — if only I just had more of this, or less of that, *then* I'll have a great life. The ego struggles to force its will over everything and impairs the ability to enjoy the moment. It takes you out of the moment and away from the wisdom of your true feelings. It distorts your experience of life with its fears. That is why bringing your conscious awareness back to the present moment (and to your heart) is so important. It takes you out of the insanity of the ego, at least for the moment, and a moment, especially a lot of moments on a regular basis, can go a long way!

What a liberation to realize that the "voice in my head" is not who I am. Who am I then? The one who sees that.

Eckhart Tolle (1948-), author

It is difficult in day-to-day life as an individual not to become completely *i*dentified with the voice in the head and accept it for who-you-really-are. When the ego is shouting loudest in the mind, self-worth is at its lowest or most vulnerable. This results in the self-worth being constantly in question in the mind. It is an ongoing challenge to honor and strengthen the self-worth. A strong sense of self-worth (self-love) is *vital.* With stronger self-worth, we are *not* more selfish but rather *more tolerant.* We become more other-focused and less "I"-focused than the ego would have us be. A strong self-esteem makes us less ego-based, less self-oriented, not more. Strong self-esteem makes us less preoccupied with ourselves and we feel less threatened by others. Because we know we are valuable and equal, we are not threatened to hear their thoughts and feelings. We allow others to be equally entitled to their opinions too. This helps move us as a society into the energy of allowance or wholeness which is love. We can then move as a community towards true equality and democracy for all. We are then better able to use the power of love and our values, not the force of our might, for the good of our own lives and for everyone else's.

Emotion generated from the fear-based, past-based, ego-based mind can be very toxic to the body over time as you can well imagine. The good news is if you recognize the ego as the illusion that it is, *the illusion ends.* Silencing ego is *not difficult.* You are *not* your mind. Also, when you bring your mind back to the present moment, ego abates. It is not hard to diffuse the mindset of the ego. However, it is difficult to keep it that way. Before long, ego fights to control your thoughts once again. Ego fears — who am I if I am not *about the past?* But *you* do not dwell in the past, only ego does. The ego is not in *actual* reality, it is caught in illusion. Your soul resides in actual reality. Your soul is all about *now.* Who-you-really-are is about now. Your true feelings are now. Peace, happiness, gratitude and love are found in the now because *you* are now. In actual reality, there is only *now.* The mind is bound by the perception of linear time. But even from the perspective of linear time, as stated previously, the past no longer exists and the future does not exist yet. It truly makes no sense to dwell in the past or the future. But the ego makes *no sense* — it is *nonsense. Now* is where it is at (and where the ego *isn't!*) *Now* holds the key to peace, happiness, satisfaction, love — the true feelings of your heart and soul.

The ego is an aspect of the evolution of consciousness. If you are thinking that mankind needs to evolve out of the ego — and fast! — you are not alone. The ego is ugly. The ego is insane. It can be monstrous. A lot of harm is done to ourselves, each other and the planet from the perspective of ego-based thinking. We keep forgetting what we have learned and continue to repeat the same insane actions of the egoic mind. As a species, we need to *wake up* to ego and *snap out of it!* But as with all things on this planet of duality, ego serves a purpose at the other end of the continuum. We are all one energetically, but we experience individuality because of the ego. Individuation is presently an essential aspect of growth and expansion as the Universe evolves through the creations that each individual is making — in their own unique way. Perhaps humanity will soon evolve beyond the ego and ego will go the way of the dinosaurs. Perhaps this will come about more readily the more we realize — in the very fiber of our beings — that we are all one. And life will evolve nevertheless without the ego-based sense of "I" — perhaps beyond our greatest dreams for a more benign way of life. But until then, the ego serves the purpose of providing a contrast. It is a powerful reminder of what humanity does not want, until we can *re-mind* ourselves to drop the ego!

The journey of the soul

The mind and soul are co-creating your physical experience. The mind is only an infinitesimal aspect of the consciousness that you really are. The soul or spirit is an aspect of the Source of it all. Unlike the mind, the soul knows how to flow with all of life. It is both here-and-now, and higher reaching, beyond this time-space-physical reality. Coming from the perspective of the All-That-Is, of the absolute, the soul knows no "other", no fear, no threats, not superior or inferior, no rejection, no lack of anything. The soul is all about experiencing the present. It is not trapped in relative concepts (e.g., past and future time) or illusions of any sort. *It is pure potential.* It can create anything in the world and has all the time (and therefore all the patience) in the world to do it! Unlike your mind, your soul knows the Grand Scheme of All Things and the Big Picture of *You.* Your mind does not know it all, which is why it is vital to tune into the wisdom of your heart (which houses the guidance of your soul) and not let the ego-based mind take over your life — which will quickly lead to disharmony in the tri-part being that you are and you will not feel good.

Your soul knows exactly what it is doing and its purpose for being here on the Earth plane even if you (in your mind's identity of yourself) do not. Your soul never forgets the higher qualities of consciousness and never strays from its course. Your soul knows your worth and holds great love for you. Your soul chooses amongst the endless variety and variations on the theme which life here offers. All of its choices are in alignment with your core values and what who-you-really-are wanted to experience and learn while you are here. Your soul will continue to offer its guidance to you and remind you of why you are here via your true feelings, for all the days of your life. You are never without the wisdom and love of the center-of-consciousness or soul that you are.

Your soul and mind orchestrates the power of the Universe to bring the events, circumstances and the people you need to create the life you choose, and to grow and expand all that you are, and all that life is, in the process. Your soul has every intention that this journey of yours be full of joy. It could not wait to get here — to Earth and this physical experience — and start to create a new grand and glorious version of you on this part of its journey. Focus on the qualities of the soul. Be vigilant with your mind when you notice it dwelling on thoughts about the past or future, fears or lack. Bring it back to now where it is easier to find relief from pain and other discomfort. *Now* is where peace and love reside. *In this moment right now* is when the full impact of your spirit, of the real magnificence of who-you-really-are, the full power of Source, can come to bear on your being.

Health, happiness and joy in life requires a balance between all aspects of your being – mind, body and soul. There are no true divisions. If you focus on well-being in any one aspect without paying equal attention to the well-being of the other aspects of yourself, something will always elude you — be it health, growth, self-worth, peace or a sense of fulfillment in life. Embrace all aspects of your being as you bring your focus back to this moment and to love and appreciation for everything that is good about your life. In this state of love and appreciation, all aspects of your being will be in harmony and can act as one. In this feeling-state, astonishing things can occur!

❧ ❧ ❧

Chapter Four

HEALTH AND THE MIND-BODY-SPIRIT CONNECTION

T he incredible diversity, function and intelligence that is life all around you is rivaled only by the incredible diversity, functioning, and intelligence that is life *within* you. At the level of matter, you are a composite of an estimated 50-75 trillion cells, all coming from a single cell, which have organized themselves into tissues and organs functioning together in one symbiotic symphony — truly a feat of intelligence of miraculous proportion. As with outer space, inner space is vibrating with the energy that gives birth to matter. Like a river, unseen intelligence is coursing through your veins. Your body is never the same way twice. It is as fluid and changeable as water itself — which is the most flexible substance of all and makes up over 50% of the adult body. Your mind is approximately 75% water. Therefore, it has the potential to be very flexible and changeable. (Remind your mind and ego of that!)

As with outer space, inner space is vast. It is not a lifeless void but rather it is alive with intelligence. It is the Source of all life expressing itself *as you*. Inner space is the starting point for everything that exists in the relative world in your body. You connect with inner space, the stillness, or Source energy, without conscious awareness of it, every time you think. Thoughts and feelings emerge from the stillness within. Like atoms materializing from the "nothingness" of outer space, neuropeptides, tiny chemical messengers in the body, spring out of nowhere in inner space. Out of the so-called void, at the very instant you think "I am happy" or " I am sad", your thought materializes into a tiny bit of matter — the neuropeptide. The neuropeptide is an extremely small protein-like molecule used by neurons to communicate with each other. In the world within, intelligence has learned to materialize into amazing, precise and powerful organic particles.

Thoughts and emotions function as cellular signals. They translate information into physical reality — mind is literally transformed into matter. Thoughts and feelings materialize into organic molecules which are capable of communicating the essence of your thoughts and feelings to every cell of your body. Neuropeptide molecules link your thoughts and emotions to every part of your body. If you are happy, each one of your 50+ trillion cells learns of it in a flash and joins in! If you are sad, angry or frightened, every cell in your body knows about that too. Thoughts and emotions are the points of connection between mind and matter — going back and forth between the two and influencing both.

The moment in time when the neuropeptide springs forth out of the void is just as inexplicable as when the first subatomic particle appears out of empty space. The human brain transforms its thoughts and feelings into thousands of chemicals every second. Wow! The neuropeptide springs into existence with the stimulation of a thought, but where it comes from—i.e., the underlying process of how the mind-body goes from *no* molecules to *one* molecule—is not known. The discovery of the neuropeptide, or messenger molecule, has served to advance our knowledge of the "oneness" between mind and body. Modern scientific understanding of brain chemistry has allowed for monumental advances in pharmacology which greatly reduces suffering to man. However, identifying the chemistry of a given state in the body is not establishing its source.

Now we are back to one of the Great Mysteries of Life that the mind cannot yet fully comprehend. We are back in the domain of higher consciousness, of invisible intelligence, the realm of the soul and of who-we-really-are. The mind-body connection i.e., the connection between a higher phase of energy (thought) and a lower phase of energy (physical matter), may be invisible but it is real. Once again, the study of quantum physics helps to bridge the gap in our understanding. The science of the invisible and surreal provides some foundation for us to begin to fathom the mystery of how something like a neuropeptide can be created out of nothingness—where nothingness is actually the silent intelligence of life waiting to materialize, the *pure potential* where matter and molecules spring from. Nevertheless, the answer to how the body goes from no molecule to one molecule—i.e., from thought and feeling to material reality—is not yet known. *But what is clear is that thoughts and feelings are the precursors to much of what gets manifested biochemically into physical reality in the body.*

The answer to the question—*How exactly* does the mind produce change in the physical body?—would be the breakthrough in healing mankind is looking for and needs. Drug therapy is not always effective or free of side effects. The human body is under increasing duress and challenge to stay well in today's world. Again, the mind of man needs to take its next step in the realm of the not-yet-believable, the "not-yet-scientific". Science needs to look to the realm of higher consciousness and the body-mind-soul connection to find the answer to healing the body. Eventually, science will prove wrong the doubting mind that says "it is not possible" or "it cannot be true". But right now, mankind is truly in need of a quantum leap in how we heal the body. This can only come about if we change how we view the body in the first place and shift our focus in the direction of the mind-body-spirit connection. Eventually, as new knowledge unfolds from this shift in perspective, the mind will look back and see how truly scientific the apparent "unscientific approach" was! What about *your* mind? Are you ready to take a leap of faith in your approach to health and healing and try something new?

Even though we may not know the mechanism of action for years to come, if ever, we know enough at the present time to know the importance of harmony and balance between your thoughts, true feelings (i.e., heart wisdom or self-worth—the domain of the soul) and your actions/choices to the health of your body and for your well-being in general. We are slowly getting clearer on what works to heal the body, although we still have a very long way to go. Not all essential information can be observed in the laboratory or confirmed by statistical analysis. Not all aspects of illness and recovery can be reduced to objective facts verified by strict scientific method or double-blind studies. When it comes to individual human beings and their health, objective reality and subjective reality are inseparable. Take the example of the placebo effect. Sugar pills should not produce an observable cure (objective) and yet they most certainly can and do if the individual believes they are the real drug (subjective). Science has shown us the powerful effect of the subjective—what a person believes—in the case of the placebo effect time and time again. The power of *belief* to invoke a cure is not only undeniably evident, it is quite elegant — placebos are non-invasive and side-effect-free. Placebo effects are a powerful example of the fact that *where the mind goes, the body will follow*.

Another example of the role of subjective factors in a person's health is evident in the occurrence of contracting a disease. The notion that disease is caused by objective, observable agents, is only partly true. A disease cannot take hold without a host who accepts it. Many who are exposed to a flu virus will not end up coming down with the flu. That outcome is determined by so much more than objective agents within the body. A person is someone who eats, drinks, thinks, experiences, emotes and believes. A person's state of balance or harmony between all aspects of their being (mind, body and soul) determines whether one is sick or well.

If we elevate the conventional scientific approach to the pedestal-position of the final arbiter of our sufferings and cures — we loose. This approach discards the wisdom of previous ages that emerged from espousing the position that the mind-body-spirit cannot be sepa-rated. We will not find the answers to the problems we face regard-ing our health if we are too busy looking primarily at the genome, DNA and other physical structures to the exclusion of other integral considerations.

In the case of chronic disease or other chronic health problems such as cyclical back pain, modern science tells us as much about their cure as a single brush stroke tells about the beauty of a masterpiece oil painting, or as a single note tells about the magic of a symphony. The beauty of music and a painting cannot be found in a single detail of it. A Big Picture perspective is needed to truly capture its essence and the magnificence of the whole of it. The same can be said about the human body. Today's trend in medical science is to treat each system separately. We must consult with a variety of specialists if we have more than one problem. We cannot compartmentalize the body neatly into systems or organs and hope to understand it all. Every system is interconnected. Every cell is interconnected by intelligent energy coursing through the body. Modern science confines its understanding of the body to a narrow or limited realm in looking for answers to problems. We need to take the Big Picture perspective of who-we-really-are in order to access the wonder of the *whole* of us and the answers to healing and staying healthy. The challenge in front of us is to attempt to better understand the intricate balance of the relationships amongst the psyche, soma and spirit. We cannot do this with traditional thinking.

The intelligent mind–body

The mind and body connection is very much a mystery. The gap between the knowledge medical science provides and how exactly the two function together is great. We do know that the mind and body are steeped in an underlying intelligence—an intelligence that allows, in the healthy body, mind and matter to coexist with each other without mistakes. Silent intelligence is at work everywhere in the natural world. In the healthy body, we all navigate this silent intelligence without even thinking about it or knowing how we do it. The body has an incredible built-in ability to self-organize, self-regulate and self-heal. The whole body is a *thinking* body. Each cell is intelligent and communicates with every other cell in a biochemical language that we can only partially explain.

The body knows what is happening to it as a whole as every cell has receptors for messenger molecules. (This is why a drug designed to treat one system can have a significant impact on other bodily systems as well.) We know the body operates with a series of chemical signals, but we do not know *what signals the first signal*. We know how cells replicate, but we do not know what signals the process of replication to begin. *What signals the brain?*

The intelligence of the body is so changeable, so quick and on-the-move that we more resemble the water we are primarily made of than solid matter. The body does not stand still to be studied. Our whole physiology can be transformed in seconds—as quickly as the chemical messengers can circulate. Change is the way of all life and the body is no exception. Atoms pass freely through cell walls and by that means you acquire new bones, new organs and new skin in a matter of months. Cells replicate constantly. Within your brain, the cells are not replaced when they die, however the content of the elements they contain (carbon, nitrogen, oxygen etc.) will be different within a year. The process of the replication and replacement of your cells, the building blocks of your body, is overseen by an invisible intelligence. Your appearance stays the same, but in actuality the body is different.

Intelligent life force is present everywhere in the body. It orchestrates our healthy functioning in a vastly superior way to any substitute we may ingest or administer. It oversees all inner events, all ongoing changes; otherwise we would be a mess of matter! Every cell can think. Your entire physical body, the matter that you are, is a result of your thinking. The mind is not confined conveniently to the brain. The mind *thinking* is projected everywhere in inner space. The body mirrors any mental or emotional event. You are what you think (consciously and unconsciously). You are what you believe. Your health is a reflection of the workings of your mind, in connection with the journey of your soul, and your emotions which bridge the tri-part being that you are! Wow! There are no true divisions. We have *invented* the separations between body, mind and spirit. All aspects of your being operate as a whole. When the intelligent energy of the body goes awry, *it* and *you* need to be treated *as a whole*. Remember the words of Plato, "The part can never be well unless the whole is well".

Conscious thought affects DNA

The intelligence of the body is what allows the body to be so fluid and flexible. While it looks like there are solid or rigid boundaries or aspects of the body that are inflexible or unchangeable, there aren't. Boundaries are illusions between single cells and organ systems. Also, there is no true or solid boundary between the body itself and the outer environment it finds itself in. The distinction between "inside the body" and "outside the body" is false. Our nervous systems register it all. An interesting study showed subjects a film of people running a marathon while monitoring a number of the subjects' physiological responses (e.g., heart rate, electrical muscle activity, blood pressure etc.). They found that the bodies of those *observing* the marathon responded in many ways identical to those who were actually running the marathon, even though they had not moved off their chairs! (Think of what watching television shows and movies can do to your body next time you are making your selection.) The boundaries within and without are not what they appear to be. Our outer environment plus our inner "environment" — attitudes, beliefs and experiences — all influence the physical body, every single cell of it.

In the world within, one of these "boundaries" or fixed, hard rules is thought to be imposed by your genes. It is commonly thought that the programming of genes will dictate or predominate, without exception. While it is true that some of our genetic programming will inevitably be expressed e.g., you may inherit brown eyes by a dominant gene for eye color, it is also true that much of it will not be expressed.

Genes only affect you if they are switched on. If they are switched off, they have no effect. Biologists used to claim that the genetic profile we are born with is fixed and unchangeable. But this claim is old science. We now know that genetic expression can be altered. Some genes can be switched off or on depending upon a person's experiences, beliefs and lifestyle choices. True to the fluid nature of the rest of the body, it turns out that the DNA of your genes, the aspect of the body widely thought to be most stable or "cast in stone", is incredibly flexible. The biological code of life is a fluid ever-changing message. Perhaps this should come as no surprise. Life — which includes genes — is always on a trajectory of change. Life is always on its way to becoming the next grander version of itself.

> *Your children are not your children. They are the sons and daughters of Life's longing for itself. They came through you but not from you and though they are with you yet they belong not to you.*

Kahlil Gibran (1883-1931), poet, author

Evidence of the fluidity of the genetic code is provided by various studies. Identical twins that are born with the same set of genes are found to have vastly different genetic profiles in late adulthood. This is good news as it leaves room for conscious choice and awareness to bring about change in the body. A recent study revealed that individuals who changed their diet and exercise and adopted a meditation practice were found to have changed the operation of hundreds of genes in their bodies. The "single-gene theory", the idea that there is but one gene responsible for a given trait such as obesity or temperament has been all but abandoned. While some traits are expressions of a specific gene, like eye color, many are not. Even aspects of the body that you think must surely be genetically fixed by a single gene, like a person's height, for example, are not. Scientists now estimate that anywhere from 20 to 100 genes are involved in determining how tall someone may grow up to be, and agree that a substantial degree of variance in the height of a person—some estimates are as high as 70 percent—is accounted for by factors other than their genetics.

The bottom line is you are born with some biological predispositions that determine some features of your body. Your behaviors will not affect certain genes, but will have a strong effect on others. Both nature and nurture play a crucial role in the functioning of your DNA. These findings allow for tremendous room for change in the body and are consistent with the characterization of it as a fluid, ever-changing stream of intelligent energy. As you bring your own preferences, passions, choices, experiences and habits into the mix, aspects of your body can change dramatically. *Your decisions affect your DNA. Conscious thought can change aspects of your genetic functioning.* Your choices play a part in the body *you* create.

The "impossible cure"

In the case of so-called "impossible" or "miracle cures", we see an incredible example of where the subjective reality of belief and objective or material reality are linked. Humanity stands in awe and disbelief in the face of such cures which defy any objective, conventional scientific explanation. Yet such cures do happen. Studies of spontaneous cures of cancer have found that in almost every case, just prior to the appearance of the cure, patients experience a dramatic shift in conscious awareness or perspective which is best described as being "beyond the intellect", at the true feeling level, which is the realm of the soul. They report a certainty or "absolute knowingness" (in every fiber of their being) that they will be cured. Some state that they feel a curative force within their body but not limited to their body—rather it extends beyond them, throughout all of nature. They report a power-ful awareness that they are part of all of existence. This apparent leap to a higher level of conscious awareness — a higher level of vibration where loving energy flows freely — prohibits the existence of disease. The cancer cells literally rapidly disappear, or at least stabilize without causing any more damage to the body.

These individuals have somehow accessed a level of intelligent energy residing beyond what we can detect or quantify. They have accessed the Source of the All-That-Is, the One Consciousness, the point of pure poten-tial where all is possible, where all of creation comes from. Recall that quantum physics tells us that creation flows from the top down, from higher energetic vibration to lower vibration, from conscious thought or awareness to matter (the body). (Note: "Thought" and "Awareness" are interchangeable terms. Consciousness = Thought = Awareness = Energy. However, consciousness can also extend to levels higher than thought. That is, it can surpass the reaches of the thinking mind where energy is vibrating at an even faster speed. As stated in Chapter One, thought is an aspect of consciousness. Thought cannot exist without con-sciousness, but consciousness does not need thought for it to exist.) The body is energy and energy is altered by thought (thought is energy at a higher vibratory level than the physical matter of the body). The impos-sible or miracle cure stems from a shift in conscious awareness which in turn shifts unhealthy or distorted energy patterns. The shift in con-sciousness unblocks or restores the flow of healthy energy in the body.

Other impossible cures share mysterious origins, e.g., faith heal-ing and placebos. In all of these cases, *a change in thought or awareness promoted a quantum leap in the body's healing mechanisms.* How extraor-dinary ordinary life really is! Old science says this is not possible. Mainstream medicine turns a blind eye to these very real cures for lack of the ability to explain the process. But the simple truth is *your state of mind determines how well your cells function.* When we look at life from the quantum perspective, from cutting-edge science, we find new foundations of thought which enables the mind to start to comprehend how this statement could possibly be true—how the impossible is not impossible at all. *Conscious awareness can restore a healthy energy flow in the body, which in turn heals the body.* This is the simple and elegant truth of healing. Would we have expected anything less from the Source of it all? Simple and elegant? Yes. Easy to achieve and maintain? No, because the conscious mind does not know how to flow very well with life. Healing requires keeping an *eye* on your *thoughts*.

Conscious awareness—do not underestimate the power of the force

Thought is one of the manifestations of life. It is a higher phase than matter with a higher vibration. Thought (or awareness) is energy and it is far from passive. Thought also creates emotion—energy in motion. The power of thought or awareness is like the power of a drug. Both thought and drugs are forms of energy and both have an impact on the physical functioning of the body. Both alter the energy patterns or flow of energy in the body. Thought creates meaning—it "speaks volumes" and it speaks directly to your cells. Remember, thoughts and feelings are at the junction point between mind and matter functioning as cellular signals. A change in thought or awareness will change the body. For example, if you imagine slicing open a juicy lemon and biting into it, you will likely start to salivate even though you have not actually put any lemon in your mouth. Your thoughts created a physical response in your body. Do not underestimate the impact of this force within you! The power of awareness lies in the fact that your body responds to it, and not just in a small way. The smallest change in awareness—the meaning of a few spoken words or a single thought — can create a huge shift in the energy and functioning of your entire body.   Notice the energetic response in your body when you imagine hearing someone tell you any of the following, for example: congratulations, you've got the job; you are fired; you are beautiful; you are stupid; you are loved; someone you love has just been rushed to the hospital.   Awareness can instantaneously change healthy energy to unhealthy energy, and vice versa.   Mind and body are one.

When we lack awareness, we get caught up in conditioning or habit.   This results in the body being on autopilot — which is equivalent to saying the energy patterns of your body become fixed.   Habits are powerful.   They create patterns that the body will follow over and over.   That is fine if your habits (including your thinking and emotional patterns) are positive or healthy.   If you do not make the connection between your thoughts and feelings, the energy that they are, and the impact that they have on the energy that is your body, you will be stuck in a battle with your body.

Mobilizing the curative power of consciousness or awareness is not as difficult as it may sound.   Maintaining it is the hard part.   Every time you change your thoughts or you make a new decision or lifestyle choice, you shift your conscious awareness which affects the energy flow in your body and the functioning of each one of your 50 + trillion cells.   For maximum well-being, it is vital to both shift your awareness and the choices you make in ways that will promote healthy energy flow.

The healing power of consciousness—may the force be with you

Intelligent healing processes are happening all the time in the body. The body successfully fights bacteria, viruses, toxins and carcinogens on a regular basis. The body heals cuts and mends bones. We do not call this impossible or miraculous. We call it natural. Perhaps we downplay the incredible feat the body accomplishes in staying healthy because we are not conscious of it. And, we tend to take good health for granted. Spontaneous or miraculous cures are the result of a natural process somehow magnified many fold. This healing process is not mystical or random at all if it can be *consciously activated or magnified*. But how do we do that?

We may never know how to consciously "throw the switch" and be transported into the realm of higher consciousness and free-flowing, healing, loving energy to obtain an instantaneous cure. And while that would be truly miraculous, we do not have to be able to do this to promote or stimulate the healing powers of the body. While making a jump to a higher level of consciousness (or somehow flowing with the consciousness of All-That-Is) seems to be a key ingredient in healing— this jump does not have to occur all at once. *A shift to higher consciousness or a shift in consciousness can be gradually and deliberately cultivated.* Nor does one have to reach a level of consciousness beyond what is typically possible to do in every day life for it to be an effective facilitator of healing. Remember, *consciousness is love.* We do not know the precise mechanism of action whereby consciousness or love, can heal. But the good news is, although we may not know how it is done, the body does! However, we need to provide the body with greater levels of the fundamental ingredient, love. Love—the soul or spirit within—needs to be fostered as the mind can do a good job pinching us off from it.

What we need to do is to assist the body by getting the barriers to natural healing out of the way and by doing all we can to foster an inner state of higher consciousness and healthy awareness which is conducive to healing. We do know something about how to do that. We remove energy blocks and restore a healthy flow to distorted energy patterns when we bring our tri-part being into balance, into harmonious alignment. And we do that by the various ways being discussed in this book, including: building emotional health through self-inquiry (i.e., pursuing an awareness and understanding of psychological patterns so that healthier patterns and self-worth [self-love] can be fostered — discussed later in this chapter), focusing on the quiet within (i.e., meditation — discussed next), following the heart's wisdom and intuition, and by making healthier lifestyle choices which love and honor the body.

Every time you follow a course of action in alignment with your self-worth or personal growth, the energy that you are shifts such that you then vibrate more in harmony with the energy of the higher qualities of your soul or the loving, revitalizing energy of higher consciousness. The energy that is *you* can then flow more freely and you will experience the benefits of this in your entire being. This is the same as saying an awareness of self-worth heals and restores you, following your true feelings heals and restores you, as does laughter, kindness, balance, allowance or wholeness, love, time in nature and meditation. All are qualities or aspects of higher consciousness. Your shift in conscious awareness to any of these states (e.g., allowance, self-worth, laughter, kindness, love) serves to shift the energy of your being which facilitates the body's intelligence to heal or revitalize itself. And every attempt (i.e., each and every time you shift back to the center, back to allowance, back to wholeness, back to love) adds up! The key is to pursue these states on a regular (preferably daily) basis so that the restorative effects can accumulate.

There is so much you can do to cultivate the healthy flow of energy within and through you. You can also go with the flow by taking the time to *not do* anything and just *be.* Each step brings your tri-part being closer to harmonious alignment, harmonious vibration. *Harmonious flow of energy, the energy higher consciousness brings, heals and revitalizes the body.* Remember, the healing vibration of consciousness is not just at the loftier heights but is available to you every time you bring your awareness back to now, back to wholeness (i.e., back to the center of the continuum), back to love. The loving energy of your soul is here for you and healing for you, right now.

Meditation—the healing effect of *going with the flow*

With growing focus on the question of natural healing, we are learning more and more about what works, even though we may be uncertain of why or how it works. One area, which is not new at all but has been the subject of renewed interest and scientific study in relation to its power to heal the body, is meditation. Meditation, also referred to as focused or conscious awareness, is not something that Western society is accustomed to but it is gaining in popularity. Perhaps this is because people are more aware of the negative impact of stressful life-styles and societal influences on their well-being and they are searching for ways to relieve tension physically, mentally and emotionally. Other reasons an individual may take up meditation is because they are feeling overly anxious, they are ill or in pain and seek some relief, they would like to slow things down as they feel like life is passing them by, or they would simply like a greater sense of peace in their daily lives. Meditation is a useful and powerful tool because it can facilitate healing and revitalize each aspect of your tri-part being. It is a good way to slow and calm down, and reach a more harmonious and peaceful state.

What is meditation? It is not "thing" you achieve, but rather a process. It is the process or practice of *allowing what is*. Meditation is allowing what is. Or, to put it another way, meditation is about paying attention, or being mindful of what is. During meditation, because the mind wanders, one needs to bring the mind back to focus on the moment, which is why meditation is referred to as a "practice"; one "practices just being". Mindfulness, a term often used interchangeably with meditation (i.e., meditation is an example of being mindful), is about paying attention or focusing on the present moment, or *allowing* what is, in the present moment.

Although there are many variations on the theme, there is no one right way to meditate. Arguably the most common method of meditating is to sit down and in a relaxed yet alert state, focus on your breath. Or, if you choose, you can focus your attention on a specific object, the environment in front of you, or a mantra (i.e., a word or phrase, such as "peace" or "I am" or "ohm", the purpose of which is to give you something to keep your attention on). The central notion is to focus your attention on what is (e.g., your breath or your mantra) and when the mind inevitably wanders, you bring it back to your present focus, without judgment of your thoughts or criticism for wandering off. As discussed previously, when you bring your awareness to something and allow it to be, without judgment, you shift to the middle of the continuum, to the place of wholeness, which is the place where love or the consciousness that is *you*, your soul, resides. This is why regular mediators describe the meditation process as "it feels like coming home". When the mind shifts to allowance, your entire being is shifted into a higher, healthier energy.

The practice of focusing on your breath (or what is, without judgment) results in a powerfully restful state for the body, while remaining awake and alert. Meditation has been described as "resting in yourself". By shifting to this fully restful state, you are better able to heal, energize, integrate and assimilate learning, and access intuition and creative ideas from higher consciousness. Our beings are whole by nature, but our energy gets distorted or blocked by lots of negatives e.g., stress, criticism, anxiety, pollution, unhealthy food etc. We need a way of restoring the healthy flow of energy to the body, and the rest of our tri-part being.

Generally, people are not practiced at focusing their inner aware-ness (which is what meditation is about) or attempting to consciously utilize or cultivate its power. Visual imagery (i.e., visualizing a healed aspect or state in the body) is an example of focused awareness without the feeling of accessing higher consciousness — but even that has been known to have a beneficial effect on the body. Meditation is a way of deliberately accessing and enabling the flow of consciousness, the flow of intelligent healing energy in the body.

In the search for ways to achieve natural healing, meditation has been shown to have beneficial effects on the body, sometimes so remarkably that it has taken researchers by surprise. You may be famil-iar with some of the findings from studies conducted on Yogis who are highly trained in meditation. While in a meditative state, some such individuals are capable of lowering breathing rates and metabolism to dramatic lows and thereby exist on little food or oxygen for prolonged periods of time. Meditation brings about a hypo-metabolic state or overall slowing down of body systems. Some interesting findings of late have shown that a regular meditation practice increases activity in the parasympathetic nervous system thereby improving blood flow and relaxation, and lowering the fight-or-flight anxiety response, levels of stress hormones, heart rate and blood pressure. As the mind and body quiet and relax, energy can flow better and the mind, body and spirit that you are can better achieve a harmonious energetic balance.

Several studies have supported the healing benefits of regular meditation practice with individuals who have chronic pain or illness.

(Note that healing does not necessarily mean curing.) Healing involves the creation of a new way of looking at or experiencing illness or disability. Healing requires coming back to center and looking at the problem from a perspective of wholeness. This allows one to let go and come to terms with things the way they are. This awareness shifts the energy of the body. It allows one to see their problem through new eyes. With daily meditation practice, while their chronic conditions were not cured, patients reported relief from physical and psychological symptoms. They experienced their condition more favorably i.e., they reported less pain, reduced anxiety and symptoms of depression, better sleep and an overall experience of a better quality of life.

There is a growing body of evidence which supports the idea that meditation is a powerful technique for restoring harmony to your tri-part being if you are unwell, and for maintaining that balance if you are well. If you are physically ill, I am not advocating that you just "sit around meditating, waiting for a miracle to heal you", as skeptics may say. I am saying that meditation is one of a number of healthy steps you can adopt as part of your daily practice to cultivate the healing power of higher consciousness and to bring your tri-part being into balance. And, it is a potent, natural restorative technique, which is often overlooked or negated by Western medicine. But to reap the benefits, one needs patience and a regular practice of meditation or mindfulness.

When you practice focusing on your breath, you will notice a flood of thoughts from your mind. In Zen tradition, this is called "watching the waterfall". It is estimated that the human mind generates on average 40,000– 60,000 thoughts per day. Wow! Meditation is *not* about stopping the mind from thinking—that cannot be done! But it does afford one the opportunity to *observe* the flood of thoughts the mind perpetually drowns one in. Once you are aware that your mind has taken its focus off the breath and has wandered off into its own world (literally), you gently, without judgment or criticism of yourself, bring the mind back to focus on the breath. Meditation is the practice of returning the mind's focus over and over again, to the present moment, or in the case of this example, to the breath. The meditator observes without judgment any thoughts, emotions, sensations in the body, and perceptions as they arise moment by moment. Meditation is the practice of being in the present moment, *on purpose*.

With regular meditation practice, the flow of thoughts may slow down a bit but it does not stop. Paradoxically, even though the thoughts keep coming, one feels as though the mind has quieted. Which raises the obvious question, how can one achieve peace and calmness with all that chatter coming from the mind? The answer is that meditation does not suppress thinking—it surpasses it! The process of meditation results in your continuously observing yourself. As discussed previously, when you observe yourself, you shift for that moment into a new perspective, the silent observer of the self, which brings a new energy i.e., you shift to the perspective and energy of consciousness. When you observe your thoughts and have become aware of your mind having wandered from the present focus on your breath, in that moment, *the mind lets go*. That momentary awareness brings about a shift in energy. Again and again, because the mind wanders constantly, when you bring yourself back to your breath, you bring yourself back to a fresh perspective (i.e., the perspective of being the *observer* of the mind, as opposed to being caught up in the world of the mind which is steeped in ego and fear-based thinking). This practice is good for you and over time, the benefits of it accumulate.

A regular practice of meditation (preferably daily) is a particularly important step in maintaining well-being because it helps you take the focus *off of your mind*. Meditation is not introspection or an "atypical kind of thinking". It is about "tuning in" to your self. It involves shifting to a level of awareness that is not conditioned. Mindfulness helps us to see through the autopilot ways of thinking and the stream of judgments and worries we are normally caught up in. It allows one to come back to the middle i.e., to assume the position of the observer or impartial witness which is also the position of wholeness, or love. As stated, the mind can be paradoxically both a great benefit to healing and a huge hindrance, unless you can keep your focus always on positive thoughts. And while positive thinking is a good idea, it is impossible to always do. While meditation is about focused thought, it actually has the effect of *taking your awareness off the content of your thoughts* (as you simply observe your thoughts and then let them pass). In this manner, meditation can help get you "out of your mind". It brings you to a level of awareness that is *not conditioned*. Or, to put it another way, it carries the mind beyond its problems — to a new awareness. In this new awareness or new state of consciousness, the block in energy created by the problematic mind (and the distorted feelings it generates) is removed or transcended, at least for the time being, and the free flow of the energy of consciousness is restored. This in turn shifts the body towards a healthier state. When the mind shifts, the body cannot help but follow.

You may like to try a variation on the theme of a meditation which focuses on your breath — and include a focus on love. This form of meditation may be particularly helpful if an aspect of your body is unwell and you need healing. Even if you are healthy, it is a powerful way to restore and revitalize your entire being. After a few minutes of breathing and quieting your mind as best as you can, focus in on your heart or solar plexus area. Send warmth and love to this area of your body. Or, scan this area and see if you already feel any warmth in a particular spot. Focus on this feeling. Go into it and magnify it. The goal is to feel love for your body and send love flowing throughout your entire body. Imagine a warm loving energy spreading over your entire body, bathing it in love. If you like, you can concentrate this energy on the place in your body which needs healing. (Unless you find that focusing on the trouble spot emphasizes your feelings of concern about it — then you are in fear, not love. If that happens, take your attention off the particular place in your body you are concerned about and go back to letting love wash over all of you as a whole.)

If you prefer, you can try variations of this exercise and visualize yourself being held in the arms of a loving presence, being bathed in a loving light, or being surrounded by your loved ones. The key is to try to leave your mind as best as you can (which no one can really do — so just allow your thoughts to flow by without judgment) and focus on the *loving feeling*. Breathe in the love. Fill your entire being with it. Move from the visualization into the *feeling* as best as you can. If you like, after a while, imagine this love flowing from you and traveling around the entire planet and back to you again. Try to spend some time feeling love each day even if just for a few moments. We spend too much time in daily life feeling fear, anger and other such energies. Balance the energy and bring your tri — part being into harmonious, energetic alignment by spending some time each day feeling love or warmth in your body.

Develop a regular habit of meditation or mindfulness

The mind is always carrying our attention or awareness away from the present moment. It insists on dwelling in the past or future. The mind is frequently frightened and fussy and shouting at us! As the present moment is truly the only time we have to live (as the past no longer exists and future does not exist yet), unless we make a habit of becoming mindful of the present, literally before we know it, the mind carries us away from our lives! Life starts to feel like it is going by too fast, or is simply going by and not bringing much joy. Try not to rush through some moments to get to "better" ones. Each one is a moment of your life.

If we are not giving our full attention to the moment, then we are *unaware*. To be unaware means the mind has divided our attention, which means we are not *fully present in life*. Lack of awareness narrows the experience of life. Lack of awareness keeps us from being in touch with all life has to offer. Lack of awareness also keeps us from being in tune with the body. As a result, we become less sensitive to how the body is being affected by our environment, our actions and habits, our thoughts and emotions.

On the other hand, awareness expands or broadens the experience of life. Awareness or mindfulness (being present and allowing what is) allows us to let go of the stream of thoughts without getting so caught up and driven by them. We are all too often pulled away from the moment at hand by all the doing, planning, worrying and reacting. *You* are not your thoughts! Shifting to observe yourself, shifting to awareness, makes room — room for a new perspective to come into your mind, room for you to see things differently, room to see more clearly and deeply and to see your individuality and connectedness with all of life.

Taking time to tune in with yourself results in your connecting to who-you-really-are, which is consciousness residing in the deep peace or inner space within. *You* reside in the "gap between thoughts". This space is the window to the soul, to the Source within you. It is the gateway to the field of infinite possibilities or pure potential. You can "seed" this quiet space with your intentions or prayers. And this is where your soul can "seed you" by whispering its guidance and insights into your ear. When the mind is quiet, we can hear the soul's wisdom. We say that the insight just popped into mind or suddenly out of the blue, we got it, or, we saw the light because with the mind open, more light can come into our being. Your mind's job is to keep you safe, which it does overzealously at times with its constant instructions to be concerned or on guard. Your mind thinks it knows what is important in your life. Your soul's job is to remind your mind of what is truly important in your life.

Mindfulness can take numerous forms e.g., a slow, focused walk, sitting in the garden, a sitting meditation with a focus on your breath, doing something artistic or creative, or just remembering as frequently as possible throughout your day to bring your mind back to the present moment. Add a mediation or meditative-type practice to your day. Find the method that works best for you. How will you know it is "working"? Simple, with practice, you will likely feel better afterwards—more relaxed and/or centered. You may feel a positive shift in your energy level, as though you have moved positive energy through your entire body. Or, you may find that you feel nothing in particular. Nevertheless, do your best to find some quiet time for mediation regularly, even if you can only find 10 minutes to spare. If meditation is not your thing, make a point to sit for a quiet contemplation every day (the less thinking the better!), or go for a mindful walk alone. Focus on fostering the love within and filling your body with love. Regardless of how you achieve it, your being needs peace and quiet to revitalize itself.

The natural world has restorative energy to offer you if you avail yourself of it. You do that by simply being in nature—but be quiet for some of the time! If you are walking with someone, walk in silence for 10 minutes. Ideally, walk in solitude. Unplug the music and turn off the cell phone, otherwise you'll miss being in the moment. *Doing* means you miss *being* with the rest of life all around you. In this age of technology, there is a growing tendency to avoid the quiet by plugging into some form of technical device talking at you. Sometimes, the need to be continuously plugged in is a response to feeling lonely or dissatisfied. To avoid these unpleasant feelings, you may be frequently plugging into some form of mass communication—TV, phone, internet etc. This may be satisfying to your mind, *but this is unsatisfying to your heart.* It is not a substitute for the emotional intimacy of relationships that your heart desires—both with others and with *yourself!* (Some solitude is healthy; however, social isolation is not.) *Both* the mind and the heart need to be nourished in order for the body to feel good and for you to feel happy with your life. You are a *tri*-part being; you are not just your mind!

As technology does not provide the degree of heart-to-heart connection your being requires in order to feel happy and fulfilled, reliance on it for connection produces stronger feelings of loneliness and unhappiness, which feeds the habit of plugging into technology even more, which in turn fuels feelings of loneliness, boredom and dissatisfaction with life. Instead, plug into the silence. Plug into yourself. Plug into your heart. The mind talks at you quite enough (as you'll discover if you try to meditate!) without having technology talking at you all the time. Your tri-part being needs the interconnectedness of relationships with others, but it also needs some time in quiet so that you can connect with yourself. For maximum well-being, your being needs you to spend some time in solitude, being not doing. In time, you'll relish it. You'll miss it if you don't get it. You'll start to notice that you don't feel as good overall if you don't get your quiet time.

Time in solitude with yourself and with nature is your opportunity to connect with the life that you are and with the life force all around you in the Grand Scheme of Things. It is time to spend connected with all of life through the heart, and not so much the mind. It is your time to connect with your spirit and with the Source of it all which also resides within you. It will help to *Revitalize Your Life.*

The role of emotion in the health of the mind–body–spirit

Emotions and beliefs play a strong role in whether or not we can achieve a healthy tri-part being. They directly affect overall well-being and whether or not the body can successfully mobilize and maintain its natural healing and restorative mechanisms. The idea that the body is somehow separate from the mind—that you can achieve wellness in isolation from mind-body reality—will undermine any efforts you make in the pursuit of physical wellness and happiness in life. It is vitally important to observe and address what your thoughts and emotions are all about.

Unacknowledged and/or unaddressed emotional distress translates into physical discomfort and can eventually compromise health and well-being. Discomfort or pain in the body is a message to work at becoming consciously aware of what is happening in your life and how you are truly feeling about it and yourself. It is a message to clarify your feelings and to take action in alignment with your self-worth and higher values. This may require you to speak your true feelings ("speak your truth") and take steps to resolve the situation. It also means working at becoming fully conscious of your problematic mental and emotional patterns which have resulted from prior or childhood experiences. What has happened that may have resulted in the formulation of unhealthy conclusions about yourself and the world around you? If you are stuck in emotional distress, ask yourself: What are you meant to see? How are you meant to grow from this? What is the learning embedded in this situation that you need to get? Self-inquiry is necessary to developing awareness of problematic patterns so that you can change them. You can change what you are conscious of. You cannot change what you are not conscious of!

If we are unable to clarify and speak our truth, our bodies start to "speak" it for us. For example, if you cannot say "no" in a given situation, and you need to in order to be true to yourself (which means following your heart's wisdom), your body will say it for you. And it communicates or speaks to you in a manner sure to get your attention— an uncomfortable or unpleasant feeling in your gut or solar plexus, irritable bowel, heart burn, an ache or pain, or an illness. Notice in the following examples how often the physical symptom someone may be experiencing mirrors the emotional underpinnings of their problem. If, for example, you are having shoulder pain—are you overly burdened by something, carrying too much responsibility on your shoulders or trying too hard to please? Are you having reflux trouble? If so, what in life are you having trouble "swallowing"? Eye trouble—what are you not seeing? Heart trouble—do you love yourself or do you need to change your perception of yourself or value yourself more? Foot trouble—what steps forward or action do you need to take in order to be true to yourself? Or, perhaps your shoe is too tight! The answer to the problem can be emotional or physical. Admittedly, it may not always be quick or easy to figure out, but if you take a close and thorough look, more often than not in the absence of a clear physical explanation, you will find that the problem stems from a problematic pattern in your thoughts and/or how you are handling your emotions. On one hand, the body is more complex than any "rocket science" the mind of man can produce. On the other hand, it is simplicity at its finest.

Emotional distress (which is the presence of unacknowledged or unaddressed emotions and/or not taking action which is in harmony with your true feelings) transforms into a complicated cascade of physical and biochemical responses in the body on a grand scale. Recall that emotions are electrical messages (e-motions = energy in *motion*) which the body translates into chemical and hormonal signals. Which means, by an incomprehensibly vast and complex means, every one of your 50 + trillion cells learns about your emotional state in a mere instant. Emotions influence and are influenced by the functioning of organs, immune defense, and a multitude of biological substances that circulate and govern our inner states. There is no division between the mind and body!

The cause of ill health and the maintenance of good health must be understood in the context of a person's life and all that is going on including their childhood foundations. So many factors influence mind-body-spirit wellness e.g., life history, familial emotional patterns, self-esteem, spiritual beliefs, physical and mental resources, and social and economic support. Wow! These are all factors which one needs to consider in pursuit of well-being and joy in life. If this sounds a bit overwhelming, you might like to look at it this way — there are also so many areas and avenues by which you can interject positive change into your life. And there are generally options for help and support to seek out. The energetic impact on your being of each positive step that you take accumulates and brings you closer to the mind-body-spirit harmony you are seeking.

There is a tendency for people — on the level of both the individual and the health care system in general — to downplay the role of stress in ill health. Also, stress is defined in too narrow or simplistic terms. Both of these problems are likely the result of the fact that in today's world, we are under so much stress that we don't necessarily recognize it or where it is coming from. We tend to downplay or turn a blind eye to stress, because if we were to stop and really consider the negative impact of it, we may have to change how we are currently navigating life. Stress is not just the occurrence of disturbing isolated events or sudden traumatic events. There are chronic daily living stresses that are more insidious and quite harmful in their long-term physiological impact e.g., an unhappy relationship, constant criticism or pressure, and internal devaluing of the self. Be on the look out for sources of stress in your life that you may be downplaying or denying altogether.

Individuals exposed to high levels of emotional stress since early childhood can become habituated to it, making it the *absence* of stress that becomes problematic for them because it promotes a feeling of boredom or unease. People can develop an addiction on a physiological level to the presence of stress hormones circulating through their systems. This can contribute to a person's continual engagement in melodramatic emotional states where even the lows produce a chemical "high". While swings from emotional highs to lows are inevitable in life, big swings while not "wrong" (which would be a judgment) inevitably place the body under more stress in the long run. The constitutions of individuals who are emotionally dramatic may seem to "take a beating but keep on ticking". The younger body can absorb a lot without visible signs of distress. However, the negative impact of such dramatic biochemical swings may well show up in a concrete way in their bodies later in adulthood.

Physical stress responses can be acute, as in the case of an isolated traumatic event, or chronic e.g., day-to-day distress — be it real, threatened or imagined (i.e., the fear that something distressing might happen). The body's stress reactions can be triggered when the threat is outside of conscious awareness, or even when the individual feels they are stressed in a "good way" (e.g., moving to a new home or getting married). Chronic stress can diminish an individual's pain threshold and may result in hyper-vigilance and hyper-sensitivity in the brain, resulting in hyper-reactivity of the nervous system.

Just as we have our habits, our physiology including our nervous system has its habits, too. Fixed patterns and functions in the body become autopilot and to some degree "hardened" into the physiology of the body over time. Be patient with yourself and your body if you are making changes in your behavior or lifestyle choices and you are frustrated with the lack of visible results. The body needs your loving patience. After all, it did not become the way it is overnight, nor will it change overnight.

Psychological health

Emotional or psychologically-based habits show up in the body's chemistry. This field of scientific study has been dubbed "the biology of belief". Emotional patterns we are conditioned to early in life become ingrained in the neurochemistry and response systems of the body. Experiences of our particular environment and early relationships and attachments, whether positive or negative (and there is no such thing as all positive, despite parents or guardian's best intentions), influence development and the subsequent patterns of functioning in the body. There are self-esteem wounds in even the most idyllic childhood experiences and these wounds show up in our biology. No one escapes them because there is no such thing as perfection.

Over time, cells replicate and organs replace themselves — yet a *memory* still exists undetectably in the cells. If there is a problem inherent in the cells of a given organ, it will be reproduced when the cells of that organ are replaced by the body. Science cannot point to this memory trace or explain it and it cannot be found in the DNA which houses the blueprints responsible for molecular replication. We know in the case of pain receptors, for example, the receptors undergo a "molecular learning" and can retain the memory of pain or amplify pain signals long after the physical injury has healed. Emotional experiences and perceptions of the environment are stored in cellular memory, although we have no idea of the mechanism of action. Our fundamental beliefs are rooted in early experience and become embedded at the cellular level. Even though we may not be conscious of them, they are strong influences in both our behavior and our biology, especially our physiological response to stress. I'll say it again…there is no separation between mind and body. See if you recognize any of these ingrained beliefs as your own: I have to be the strong/responsible one; if I am angry, I am not loveable; I have to be needed in order to be valuable; I have to be ill in order to deserve nurturing; I must do a perfect job or else I am a failure. *A person's deeply held beliefs have foundations in their cells.*

In order to maximize well-being, the internalized beliefs must be exposed and altered. This is the domain of psychology. A strong underpinning of psychotherapy (a generic term, meaning "talk therapy") is that you can work on/change what you are conscious of. In other words, a key to healing and wellness is an individual's *conscious awareness and free and informed choice.* That is, you are free to re-think things, or make up your own mind about the beliefs you hold about yourself and your life, *if you have awareness of them.* A goal of the psychotherapy process is to enhance your conscious awareness of yourself. Your psychologist acts like a mirror, *reflecting you* (i.e., your thoughts, feelings, autopilot habits, and beliefs) *back to you* so that you can see yourself more clearly. Having gained new awareness or *observed yourself,* you can then decide what to do about it. In this way, you can consciously liberate yourself and your biology from your beliefs and in so doing, achieve a healthier, more balanced tri-part being. Do not underestimate the healing power of conscious awareness—it can help to set you free!

How might a psychologist be of help to you?

If you are struggling in some area of your life—perhaps in your personal relationships or in your relationship with yourself—and you seek clarity and a path through it, you may wish to have some counseling. When the mind, body and spirit are not functioning in harmony, we can find ourselves caught in a vicious circle. For example, if you are feeling somewhat down, anxious or unworthy, these feelings will impact on the body, resulting in unpleasant feelings or physical symptoms such as tension, pain or illness. The more you do not feel well physically, the more you may withdraw, loose social support, not sleep well etc. which will in turn magnify depressed or anxious feelings and/or low self-worth. Before you know it, you are caught in a vicious circle. If this is happening to you, you may wish to seek the services of a psychologist. A psychologist has expertise in the areas of human behavior, mental health assessment and treatment, and behavioral change. You may benefit from the collaborative effort with such a professional who is well schooled and focused on helping you identify problematic patterns of thinking, feeling and behaving—patterns that you may be fully conscious of, have an "inkling of" or that are fully "autopilot" or unconscious.

Sessions with a psychologist should provide a supportive, nonjudgmental and confidential environment where you can talk freely and receive objective feedback. (Note: Psychotherapy or "talk therapy" can be offered by a psychiatrist or social worker in addition to a psychologist. The training of each professional is different. Look for the best fit for you. Then trust your gut feel of the "goodness of fit" in the first session or two. A good fit with your counselor is one of the best indicators of a satisfactory outcome.)

Having the benefit of objectivity and training, your psychologist can interpret and reflect back to you what information about yourself you bring "to the table" (more likely the chair or couch!) You will gain the opportunity to see yourself differently or more fully in the "mirror" of their feedback to you enabling your awareness of yourself to grow. You will decide if their feedback "fits" i.e., accurately reflects you, or not. You will know by how you *feel* and will work together until it fits. When it does, you will see yourself and your life more clearly and your self-concept will shift i.e., you will *transcend to a higher level of conscious awareness regarding yourself.* Conscious awareness is freeing and moving— you are literally moved to a higher level energetically. With a new level of awareness, you become *freed up* from old beliefs or patterns of responding which were not serving you well. You are then *freed up* from the distorted energy such problematic patterns of thinking and feeling created in your body.

I wish to clear up some popular misconceptions about psychotherapy. A typical course of psychotherapy is *not* years in length. Nor is it on average even one year in length. It *does not* have to take dozens of sessions to gain an important insight which will help to enable you to break free from problematic patterns. In fact, it does not generally take even a dozen sessions. Having said that, of course everyone's life story is unique, and some individuals may find they need or want more time to work through issues. And while long-term psychotherapy still exists and can bring benefits, it is *not* the norm. There is an important contribution necessary from both sides of the equation, the therapist's and the client's, to bear in mind in response to the question of how long one needs to be in psychotherapy in order to realize a substantive benefit. On the one hand, this is the day and age of everyone wanting it all now, or even better, yesterday. And, like everyone else, a good therapist has to be able to keep a reasonable pace with the expectations of today and do their part to provide wisdom, guidance and an overall useful experience for their clients in the short term or face going out of business. On the other hand, the client needs to do their part which means first, sticking with the process long enough to give it a chance to be useful to them and second, they must provide the vital "grist for the mill" i.e., their thoughts, feelings and experiences, as they are comfortable and able to do so. In this way, the *client* sets the pace and will greatly influence the efficacy of the experience.

If you and your therapist are a good fit, you can likely achieve some useful insight and direction to help resolve problems in just a few months, often less (sessions are typically once per week). Healing from traumatic events (e.g., car accident, abuse) will no doubt require more time. Nearly everyone reports that at least some psychotherapy is better than none. A common adage is you get out of therapy what you put into it. I like to say that the client is in the driver's seat. The therapist is following along behind, picking up the pieces the driver gives out and offering (reflecting) them back to the driver through an objective perspective (the rear view mirror!) Where the driver goes with the new insights and perspectives they now clearly see is up to him/her.

It is an equally popular misconception to think you can build your self-esteem, solve your personal relationship issues and confront your boss in three sessions or less! Some expectations for fast results are not reasonable or possible. Building self-esteem and personal growth are processes I believe we face our entire lives. But you can seek professional help and do a good "piece" of short-term work on your self-worth now. As life evolves and brings you new challenges, new opportunities to grow and acquire self-worth, you can go back to therapy and do another piece of work.

The potential healing effect of self-insight or self-awareness lies in the fact that when you transcend the mind's problematic and habitual patterns of thinking (which lowers self-worth and distorts the body's energy), you move to a higher level of consciousness. Self awareness frees you up from the conditioning of your mind and moves you to a state of higher, healthier energy. The higher vibration of healing, loving energy has a restorative effect on your entire being. In short, you feel better. The "freeing" feeling from developing self-insight results from the fact that your new awareness has produced a shift, literally, in the energy of your body. You are freed up to flow better with life. Awareness enables you to make changes to better value yourself. Self-worth = Loving Energy which revitalizes you. Self awareness enables you to surpass the level of consciousness of the conditioned mind and its frequent self-defeating habits and the distorted emotion it generates. Once you have the insights, you do not forget them. The mind is transformed by a quantum leap of new thought. The wisdom of breakthroughs is not forgotten. However, in time the mind latches on to new egoic and fear-based thought patterns, which is why I say the process of building self-worth and personal growth requires continuous conscious awareness throughout our lifetime.

Awareness created by insight has the power to *move* you

Once you gain a deep understanding of yourself in therapy, you have it and you are highly unlikely to forget what you are now fully conscious of. The effect of understanding yourself at a deeper level can be truly profound and life changing. Your enhanced conscious awareness will allow your self-esteem to move to a higher level and it will influence how you choose to navigate through life in the days ahead. Contrary to another popular thought, the role of the psychologist is not to tell you what to do, although you can count on them to help you generate some new ideas and possible courses of action. And while advice may be asked for and given, the primary purpose of psychotherapy is to provide you with *insight*. Insight is more helpful than advice. Insight about yourself has the power to transform you—*it shifts you, literally*. It *moves* you energetically speaking. You can "feel it right down to your bones" because your bones *know* it too. Each one of your 50+ trillion cells knows about it and is affected by it. You know it "in every fiber of your being". Again, there is no separation between your mind, body or soul. *Separations are imagined.* There is no "just working on your mind" or "just working on your body". What affects one affects the other. There are no true divisions!

You do not need to be in crisis (in fact it is better to seek help *before* a crisis ensues) to seek self awareness in psychotherapy. You just need to have the desire to gain a deeper understanding of yourself—and who could not benefit from that? The psychotherapy process helps in a variety of ways: you are not in the problem alone; the focus is all about you (unlike when you are talking to a friend or family member); it helps you to focus your attention and hone in on the problem areas; and it facilitates awareness, momentum, change, hopefulness, resilience and coping mechanisms, thus relieving symptoms of depression, anxiety or feelings of lack of control in your life. Wow!

If you are thinking you should be able to solve things or gain the insights on your own (a frequent comment I hear), I respond this way: First of all, you cannot see yourself from an objective perspective. (You are too close to yourself!) Second, two heads are better than one when you are trying to generate ideas. Third, your psychologist will have a great deal more training than your friend. And last but not least, they will not interrupt you and start talking about themselves on your time!

If psychotherapy is not for you for whatever reason, do your best to look at yourself with compassion and bold honesty. How might you be inadvertently undermining yourself? What mental and emotional conditioning do you need to become aware of? How have you learned to be critical and unloving of yourself? How might fears be holding you back? Look back at significant or pivotal moments in your life, the times that were difficult in particular. What conclusions did you draw about yourself then—about how to navigate through life, about the expectations you have for yourself and others? Trust your intuitive sense. Sit quietly with your questions and ask your heart's wisdom. As it is usually easier to identify someone else's problem rather than your own, you might like to ask someone close to you what they think, but do not do that unless you are prepared to be told exactly what your problem is!

In addition to looking into the mirror of yourself, if it is self awareness you seek, an important source of insight are the other mirrors in your life, namely the mirrors of a partner or some other individuals you are in a relationship with e.g., a friend or co-worker. Look particularly at the person who catches your attention or pushes your buttons the most. We project the disavowed aspects of ourselves onto the other. What you see in them is also something you need to see in *yourself!* Look closely and below the surface. What you need to see is not likely obvious at first glance. Patterns in relationships keep repeating until we get the learning and growth. Life keeps bringing us what we need to enable our own evolution.

We are undoubtedly creatures of habit—psychologically and physiologically. Mental, emotional and behavioral patterns are learned in our developmental years and are carried forward by conditioning to adulthood. These patterns may have served a useful or protective function (a psychologist would call that a defense mechanism) in childhood but they may or may not be helpful in adulthood. In fact they may be counterproductive in some way—hampering your peace of mind or sense of self worth. Whatever hampers you mentally and emotionally, will impact the energy that you are negatively. That is, it will create a block or distortion in the healthy flow of the energy of your body. What ideas or notions about your self-concept did you "lock in" deep in your mind (and consequently in your cells) as a child? For example, is your self-worth entangled with beliefs from your foundation years that you are "second best", that your feelings do not count or are wrong? Do you feel that your worth is dependent upon being the fixer, the pleaser, the peacemaker or always being perfect? Waking up to or becoming fully conscious of your patterns is crucial to breaking free of them. We are vulnerable to getting stuck in our tragedies and challenges instead of moving through them. No, moving through them is not easy, but it is more easily done with professional support and guidance than if you try to do it alone.

I firmly believe that at the core of *every* issue without exception is a self-esteem and personal growth theme i.e., an opportunity for you to foster self-worth and personal growth. Everything, every event, every relationship you have, every person you meet is a mirror — *it reflects you back to you*. Who are you? Do you know yet? What characteristics and values define you? Have you decided that you are valuable and worthy of love? Do you *feel* equal to others? Do you know what a powerful creator you are? Greater self-worth means you have a stronger more stable foundation upon which to build a happier and healthier life. We are meant to keep growing and evolving — to keep moving to higher and higher experiences which the soul calls "love" and the mind calls "life". We collect more and more incredible life experiences our whole lives. Life continuously produces an experience of who we are and an opportunity to move to the next level in your expression of yourself.

Remember, the health of your thought processes, emotional patterns and physical body are all linked. Therefore, maximum happiness and well-being in life can only be achieved by creating and maintaining a harmonious balance between all of the aspects of your tri-part being, of who-you-really-are. Your emotional health is essential to this balance. And a healthy self-worth is vital to having a good life experience.

❧ ❧ ❧

Chapter Five

SELF-ESTEEM

The essence of your tri-part being, the living glue that binds it all together, is self-love. Self-love (i.e., self-esteem or self-worth) is built by listening and following the wisdom of your soul, which comes through to your body in the form of your true or natural feelings. Your true feelings—your heart's wisdom or inner guidance system—is the wisdom of your soul or spirit. When you follow your true or natural feelings, you will find your way to self-love. Remember, life's energy or flow is always trying to bring us back to love. Self-love is the place in the center of any continuum. When we follow the path of love, the two poles of duality collapse and merge into one whole. Love is inclusive. Love is wholeness. Self-love is the allowance of *all* aspects of the self. Self-love or self-esteem is *the feeling of being equal to others (the center of the continuum), not inferior or superior (which are the two poles, or extremes of the continuum).*

Following your heart's true feelings and the higher qualities of your soul (including your values) brings you back to love. It centers you, literally. Self-love, the energy of your soul, restores the harmonious vibration of your entire being. It restores wholeness. The higher energy (faster vibrations) of your soul, i.e., love, revitalizes you and is healing to your mind and body (slower vibrations). Higher consciousness heals and restores lower consciousness. Self-love or self-esteem nourishes your mind and body as surely as the food you eat. It supplies a flow of positive energy to every cell in your body. Self-esteem is essential to physical well-being, happiness and a sense of fulfillment in life.

Given that life will always bring you back to love, life's events, circumstances and relationships with all their pluses and minuses are all *opportunities* in their essence i.e., opportunities for you to learn about yourself, expand the great "frontier" that is *you,* and grow or strengthen your self-esteem or self-love. As a result of living your life — making decisions and choices, and creating the next experience or opportunity — *the love that you are grows.* And these opportunities for your growth just keep coming, like it or not! Your mind might be happy not having growth experiences, particularly the so-called negative ones. But remember, on the soul level, nothing is experienced as negative. It is all an aspect of love (which is the sum total of all negative and positive charges) with a potential for expansion to an even higher level of love. Life is seeking the highest level of love, as is the aspect of the life force known as *you.* On the Earth plane, so-called negative experiences are particularly important for giving us a strong nudge out of "status quo" because if we stay stuck there, stagnancy and eventually entropy in this lifetime are next, as opposed to our evolution. The tri-part being that you are is always being "tugged" at by the force of life. Growth is your eternal destiny. Patterns in your life will keep repeating to facilitate your growth process. They may show up next in your romantic life, family life, work life or friendships until you "get it" — until you get the intended learning or personal growth experience (your soul knows your true intentions). That is, until you acquire the next aspect or experience of love, which is what all of life really is. Once you've reached that level of learning or that *level of love*, the next level of love or growth opportunity comes along! *You* are on an ever-ascending journey of love, or light i.e., a journey of *enlightenment*.

Moving to the next level *is* growth and growth *is always* the direction that your soul is flowing in. Your soul is patient. It knows the Big Picture of your eternal journey of growth and expansion, but your mind does not. Your soul never forgets your intentions in this physical life of yours. It endeavors to remind your mind of this always, and *all ways*. Your soul can afford to be patient, after all, it can wait *forever* for you to get it; whereas your physical body cannot and it would like you to get it sooner rather than later! So would your mind, because repeating patterns after awhile may become boring, tiresome, hurtful or worse, depressing. And that is unhealthy energy. If physical life is not moving towards growth (evolution), then it is moving towards death (entropy), until it re-materializes into its next grand version of itself. Either way, the life that you are is always moving. The absence of growth is entropy, which is distorted or chaotic energy, which means life is diminishing, folding in on itself — decaying not flourishing. This produces disharmony and results in unhappiness — the opposite of what we all want which is a tri-part being in harmony or wholeness, which brings happiness.

The spirit that you are is on a journey to higher and higher levels of consciousness. This is the same as saying you are on a journey to higher and higher levels of love. The love that *you are* is ever-evolving. The All-That-Is, which in its essence is love, is forever expanding through you and everyone else. A strong sense of self-worth is vital to your *enjoying* your own evolutionary journey. You can facilitate the journey of your soul and your experience of a happier and more fulfilled life by following your true feelings. Or you can work against yourself by tuning out your true feelings and failing to hear the wisdom of your heart and soul.

If you fail to embrace and honor your self-worth (i.e., you do not feel equal to others) or do not follow and resolve your true feelings when need be, thereby fighting against your own personal growth (which is the direction your spirit and all of life flows in) *you will not flow with life*. Your energy will become blocked or distorted. You will find that the patterns your life falls into will become boring, meaningless, depressing or frightening. Your life will fold in on itself and both your experiences and your physical body will diminish before their time.

If you are lacking in self-esteem you are vulnerable to the will of others, to their expectations of you or their view of you (whether that may be positive or negative, it is still *their* view, not your own). Lacking self-esteem brings suffering, fears and an insatiable craving for approval. It often results in our compromising our personal power and betraying ourselves because of a lack of courage or integrity.

Failing to honor the mind, body and spirit that you are by putting yourself down, not listening and following your true feelings and not nurturing or valuing yourself and your body will result in your physical health being compromised. The stress of such actions and sufferings translates into unhealthy energy in the body that is the precursor of disease. All healing techniques can offer only minimal or temporary relief from symptoms when the essential ingredient for health, self-worth, is lacking. Without the positive and transformative energy of self-worth coursing through your veins, you will revert back into the problematic patterns of thought and behavior that created the vulnerability to *dis*-ease in the first place.

If you are lacking in self-esteem (i.e., you are invested in feeling inferior or superior, the two poles of the continuum) your mental and emotional good health is also compromised. You become more vulnerable to the ego-based, fear-ridden mind and to the unhealthy energy of unresolved or distorted feelings resulting from any self-destructive "tapes" that your mind may be playing out of habit and prior conditioning.

If you are not honoring your self-worth and embracing your personal growth, the patterns in your life will keep repeating until you do—what we resist persists. Recognize patterns as a call to further growth and transformation. You can break free from unwanted patterns and blocked energy by coming back to a perspective of self-worth and personal growth. Look for the learning embedded in the situation. See how the situation is mirroring an aspect of you back to you so that you can be fully conscious of it. You can work on and change what you are conscious of. See how the circumstance is challenging you to grow and providing you with an opportunity to come back to the middle, to come back to love, especially self-love. Seek help if you are having trouble finding the growth potential. Listen to and follow your true feelings. Embrace your personal growth. Work on feeling equal. Work on treating others as your equal. Let the answer to the question, "What would self-love do?" be your guide to breaking free of the unwanted patterns and the blocked or distorted energy that these patterns (via the unwanted emotions they produce) bring to your tri-part being. Fostering self-worth or self-esteem is vital to your revitalizing your life.

🌿 *Remove those "I want you to like me" stickers from your forehead and instead, place them where they truly will do the most good—on your mirror!*

Susan Jeffers, author

How do we strengthen self–esteem?

I am indebted to the wisdom of Lynn and Bernie McKenna who co-authored the rest of this chapter with me and in so doing they add their contribution to this effort to help uplift humanity and the planet. I am also proud and pleased to tell you that these individuals are my mother and step-father, now retired from decades of serving the public through their clinical psychology and family counseling practice.

Having self-esteem or self-worth means *feeling equal*. We all agree that self-esteem exists, it is essential, it is the foundation of, and governs the quality of, our independence, personal development, achievement and our relationships, including effective parenting. On a community and national level, it is the foundation of democracy and peaceful co-existence. For decades, professionals and lay persons alike have agreed that enhanced self-worth is an important, if not essential ingredient for personal growth, achievement, or quality relationships. Self-esteem has been a subject of a great deal of focus in a multitude of studies and programs reported on by professional journals, books and the media. Headlines abound e.g., "Learn to Love Yourself", "Some Children Destined to be Bullied", "Eating Disorders Third Most Common Chronic Illness for Teen Girls", "Tasks to Aid Self-Esteem Lifts Grades". We all know it is important, we all agree that we need it, but as a society, we are unclear as to how to raise children with the foundations for strong self-esteem and to build self-esteem in adulthood.

There is wide variance amongst professionals and parents alike in their understanding of and approach to the development and enhancement of self-esteem. Some therapists give advice, some focus on symptoms rather than causes, some try to change the behavior of the person and others offer courses for self-help or for parenting. In adopting primarily an authoritative and/or rational approach, there is often insufficient emphasis on emotional content which stresses understanding and accepting the essential role of our emotions in moving toward independence—and in the extreme may foster emotional dependency, which is the very basis of low self-esteem. The parental focus is primarily on the achievement, encouragement and praise of their children. Both professional and lay approaches to self-esteem development lack an emphasis on the basics of understanding and resolving one's natural or inherent feelings in a way that promotes the individual's own autonomy and equality (i.e., emotional maturity). What does this mean and how do you achieve this? Read on!

As infants, we are born with rudimentary, security-related fears e.g., a fear of loud noise. We are helpless and completely dependent on a parent(s) or guardian for security and nurturance. Eventually, depending on the quality and consistency of the parental warmth and caring, a closeness and trust will ensue, called love. As the young child feels protected and satisfied, love will be experienced from child to the parent, the parent to the child, and eventually from the child to him or herself—the child learns they are lovable.

On the other hand, to the extent that the child's parents seem distant or inconsistent, the child will feel less protected and less trust. The child's insecurity may result in the child making efforts to cling to their parents more and/or the child may gradually withdraw, depending on the degree of perceived neglect. Rather than experiencing this mounting fear of being rejected and of being alone, the young child will often cover the fear with "guilt", and feeling unloved, will begin to blame themselves. The child will feel they are at fault. If their parents find them unlovable it must be true—they are unlovable. Although this "guilt" is not true (i.e., they have done nothing against their own values to warrant feeling truly guilty), the child will remain convinced they are not good enough and bury their fear of not being lovable, and also any anger and hurt feelings towards their parents, and instead be vaguely angry at him or herself.

As the young child moves through the toddler stage and needs and wants to explore their world, they will be profoundly affected by how their parents establish limits. The parental "No!" is echoed by the child and the contest begins. If the parent models expressing anger clearly, consistently and firmly and uses age-appropriate language that aims at correcting the behavior without attacking the child personally—and if they listen to the child with understanding but not necessarily agreeing with their outbursts—then the child feels heard and understood and gradually, by school age, is able to participate in the process of working out differences as an equal. That is, the democratic principles are upheld between parent and child—each party is entitled to their feelings, their feelings are right for them (i.e., each person's feelings are of equal value), and each person's feelings are considered in the solution. Although the parent and child do not have equal power i.e., the parent is in charge, the child is learning the rudiments of democratic communication which results in their *feeling of equal value which forms the basis of healthy self-esteem in the child.*

Democratic communication enhances self-esteem

The developing child learns that expressing anger and other underlying feelings is an important part of "fighting fairly", that his or her feelings are based on their own point of view, needs and wants and are of value to him or her, and that they are worthy of these feel-ings. The child learns that expressing their feelings is a necessary part of maintaining a close loving relationship with their family. Equally important, the child begins to practice quality listening to their parents' feelings, knows that is it all right to disagree with their parent's feel-ings, yet the parents' feelings are of equal value to the child's, and any differences are to be worked out by negotiation that satisfies the par-ents and child's *feelings* equally. The actual solution may or may not be a 50/50 compromise. But the important point here is that both parties have an experience whereby their *feelings* are considered equally, and the agreed-upon resolution works towards alleviating the feelings of both parties. (Rather than on the differing points of view, or the "right" and "wrong " of an issue, the all-important divide is due to the *unre-solved feelings* on both sides. If left unresolved, these feelings contrib-ute to low self-esteem, dependency and distance between loved ones.) This is the process of fighting fairly i.e., a democratic way of resolving disagreement based on equality. As the child moves in to adolescence, they will struggle to find a balance between pleasing (loving) them-selves and their parents. This is essential for their gradual and neces-sary separation from their parents.

The democratic communication process enhances the child's love for him/herself as well as for others. If, in addition, both parents model expressing their feelings, quality listening, and resolving their differ-ences openly between each other, this whole process is reinforced. Of course the parents will need to use discretion in exposing their children to the process of resolving disagreements between themselves, but it is important that the basic principles of fighting fair are somehow mod-eled to the child when appropriate, or if not directly modeled, then they can be brought up in a discussion with the child later. A child can feel tension between their parents from an unresolved disagree-ment whether or not they witness any arguing directly. You can, for example, explain to your child after the fact that you and your partner felt quite differently about something, each party's feelings are "right", and you came up with a solution which considered the feelings of each other equally (i.e., each person's feelings are of *equal value*). It is important that the child learn that adults in love disagree and when they do, their feelings are of equal value and they need to listen to each other and consider each other's feelings equally in the resolution. Democratic communication results in the parents being closer to each other, and closer to their children who in turn are equipped to model in the future fair or democratic fighting (based on equality of feelings) as adults to their children.

Of course no child receives the perfect balance of unconditional love and consistent, appropriate limits. No parent has received this from their parents. There is no such thing as perfect parenting. As a result, children inevitably experience degrees of fear of being unloved and alone and at times feel hurt that they are indeed unloved, or alone. In addition, at times they experience hurt because a parent is feeling hurt. This is a hurt resulting from loving and empathizing with their parent i.e., "I feel hurt because you are hurting."

Due to the magnitude of these deep feelings of fear and hurt, we learn to cover them with defenses of angry outbursts, silence, withdrawal or acting out. As we mature, we probably realize to some degree that these are childish or immature ways of avoiding our true feelings, and we may then feel guilty (anger at ourselves) for avoiding our feelings and/or rebelling (which often results in hurting others). This is true guilt to the extent that we are aware of our immature avoidance of feelings and acting out or withdrawal. When we learn to express this guilt and change our habits by openly admitting this guilt to ourselves and others and change our childish behavior, we will blame ourselves less and feel more lovable. Self-esteem grows.

There are five true or natural feelings

Love, anger, hurt, fear and guilt—these are the five inherent, fundamental and essential feelings. They originate from your soul or higher consciousness (heart's wisdom) and constitute your inborn guidance system. Depending on how they are identified, expressed, valued and resolved, these true or natural feelings will affect your feelings towards yourself (your self-worth) and towards others—affecting the quality of your relationships.

> ➢ **1. Love:** I care about or value myself (self-worth) and others. That is, I value or love them for what they are and want to feel close to them. I feel **happy** when I value/love myself and others, and when *I have faced and resolved my feelings.*

> ➢ **2. Anger:** I defend my autonomy against that which seems unfair, wrong or unjust. I stand up for my rights (I am assertive) while respecting the rights of others (I am not aggressive).

> ➢ **3. Hurt:** I feel devalued or unloved when someone I care about doesn't seem to care about me. Also, I feel empathic hurt because a loved one is hurting. (Hurt may also be the result of physical pain.)

> ➢ **4. Fear:** I fear that I am not as good as others and will be rejected. In other words, I fear that I am unequal or unworthy (inferior) which is the greatest fear and at the root of the other fears. * (See Note below.) Also, I fear physical or emotional danger causing hurt.

> **5. Guilt:** I dislike a specific aspect of myself or my actions. I have gone against my principles or values (often to avoid a fear).

*Note: I wrote at the outset of Chapter Three that our soul *does not* fear we are unworthy or inferior. That is the work of the *mind.* And so, you are likely wondering — why have I listed a fear of rejection or inferiority here, as one of the true feelings originating from the *soul*? You may also recall from Chapter One, I talked about the fact that natural life on the planet of duality does not necessarily fall neatly into just one category to keep things simple for us and more readily understood. Fear of rejection i.e., of inadequacy or inferiority, is one such example.

I still maintain that the fear of inadequacy does not come from the soul. It is a product of the mind. And the mind is capable of producing great distortions of this fear. From birth, we are subject to the conditions of being a human infant i.e., we are completely helpless and dependent on our environment and the quality of parenting we get. Also, we are born into a physical body which has a fear-based, egoic mind. Because of our early dependency and ego, it is a natural product of being human (but not soul-based) to have a measure of fear of being rejected because we are unworthy. That is, we have some fear that we are unworthy or inferior *almost* from the time we are born, from very early in childhood.

Fear of rejection is an inescapable feeling for every human being; however, it varies in the *degree* to which we experience it. We all experience *to some degree* a fear of rejection from early childhood onward. For this reason, I have included it in the five true, inherent feelings. This "kernel" of fear can be pumped up (distorted) by the mind to reach significant proportion i.e., a full-blown feeling of inferiority, or it can be faced by the mind and resolved. Its resolution is essential to strengthening our self-esteem and our journey of personal growth. The degree to which we are able to resolve this almost-built-in-from-birth fear regarding our worth and prevent it from escalating will depend upon the quality of parenting, love and reassurance we received, our life experiences, and the work we do throughout our lifetime to overcome our fears of unworthiness.

All five true feelings are based on love: anger is based on your love for yourself; hurt is based on your love for another; guilt stems from the recognition that you want to be true to the loving, higher values that you believe in; fear (security fears) are based on self-love, and fear of rejection is the *absence of self-love* in that moment (when you face your fears of rejection, your self-love grows). All five feelings are positive in the sense that they are necessary for the process of personal emotional growth. When you take responsibility for your feelings, you will ease or completely resolve them. Taking responsibility means you must first identify your true feelings within yourself or "own" them i.e., become consciously aware of them. (If you are having an emotional reaction to something, work through the entire list of the five feelings above and inquire deeply within your heart — am I experiencing any of this feeling?) The next step is to face your feelings which means, in the context of a relationship, speaking them clearly and directly *out loud*. Often, this alone helps to ease or resolve them. Finally, you need to act in accordance with your feelings (which may mean negotiating a resolution which considers your feelings equally with your partner). *When you face and resolve your feelings in this manner (i.e., take responsibility for them) your self-esteem grows.*

There are many words describing feelings, yet these are "adjectives" that describe either the volume of one of the five essential feelings or some combination of the five feelings. For example, a different volume or degree of fear is described by the use of the adjectives "worried", "terrified", or "panicked". However, each adjective describes the same feeling in its essence, fear. A different degree of anger is described by the adjectives "dislike", "frustrated", "annoyed" and "furious". Each adjective denotes the same feeling, anger, just a different degree of it.

These five feelings are the "bottom denominators". (A comparable analogy is that the three primary colors — red, yellow, and blue — are the bottom denominators of color in that all other colors are a mixture or blend of these three essential ones.) They are your true or natural feelings, and their meanings are quite clear. Other words or adjectives are less clear and require further breakdown into their emotional components in order to grasp their true meaning and identify the essential feeling inherent in the expression. For example, imbedded in the meaning of the adjective "boredom", are the true feelings of fear, anger and guilt. In the adjective "happiness", the natural feeling is love (feeling lovable or loved); "rage" is the true feelings of anger, fear, and guilt; "jealousy" is the feelings of fear, anger and love; and "shame" is the feelings of fear and guilt. These descriptive adjectives generalize the feelings as opposed to being specific or accurate, and do not clearly inform the listener (your partner or yourself for that matter) what exactly you are feeling. The listener is then left to guess or interpret what you mean which may result in misinterpretation or feeling "blamed" (which is the true feelings of hurt, anger and fear).

Your true feelings—the truth shall set you free!

I stated earlier that the "opposite" (the absence) of love is not evil, but fear (fear is at the root of evil doings). Although we *are* love, the mind can do a good job pinching us off from experiencing the love that we are. That is, we forget and we doubt our worthiness. We all have a seed of fear of being rejected or of being inadequate which gets planted early in childhood simply as a consequence of being human. Depending upon the quality of love, reassurance and modeling we received from our parents, our life experiences, and our ongoing efforts to identify and resolve our feelings, the mind can guide us to face inadequacy fear as it crops up over the course of our lives and resolve it. Or, if we fail to face our fear, the mind can operate on it and distort it, causing it to grow to significant proportions i.e., a full-blown fear of inferiority is developed by the mind. On the surface, it may seem like a good idea not to face fears—after all, that is frightening! The mind tells us if we attempt to face our fear of being rejected, we could actually get rejected! Consequently, we may "hide behind", or in psychological terms, use our inferiority fear as a "defense mechanism". That is, the mind invents this defense of "I am inferior" to try to protect the self (or so the mind thinks) from having to face what is frightening. (I.e., I am inferior anyway, so there's no point in even trying to face my fears. I'll just fail, or be rejected.) On the surface, this defense may seem like a good idea (no one wants to get hurt or be rejected), and at the time, it may well be. But in the long run, as adulthood progresses, this defense mechanism eventually backfires. With the mind's defense operating, we are divested of the responsibility of managing (facing and resolving) our own feelings—in this case, an inferiority fear.

While it may be true that others have hurt you deeply in your life and perhaps rejected you, and your natural feelings in this regard (of hurt and fear) are right and true for you, it is also true that it is your *own mind* that is *now generating and hanging onto* (stuck in) the distorted thoughts and emotion that you are inferior or unworthy. As long as you avoid resolving your feelings, you and your entire tri-part being is saddled with the weight and negative energy of these painful thoughts and emotions regarding yourself.

Defenses are built over time by conditioning or "autopilot" thinking and are not in our conscious awareness. Over time, we come to believe the mind's concocted defenses are true—we're an inferior person. This may lead to blaming others for one's feelings, emotional dependency, and/or giving up on personal growth and allowing fears to dictate one's life course. *However, we can work at becoming conscious of our fear-based defenses!* And with our conscious awareness (which might necessitate some psychotherapy), the mind's distortions are exposed which weakens them or dissolves them completely. With awareness, the mind's fears or distortions fall away and no longer have a hold on us. We can work on what we are conscious of! *This is the power of conscious awareness – it is freeing.*

You get conscious of, and can free yourself up from the distortions of the mind by identifying, expressing and acting on your true or natural feelings and thereby resolve them. *This is how you strengthen your self-esteem.* This results in you growing up – emotionally! It results in you feeling *happy* or freed-up because you have cared enough about *yourself* to *own and follow your own truth.* Your love for *you* grows. And you feel lighter, because you are lighter, literally – you have opened to hold more love, which is light. It results in you feeling better physically because you have shed the burden of the negative energy created by carrying around the fear and distorted emotions. Your tri-part being is now free to flow with life and you will be a lot happier and healthier as a result. Wow! Who wouldn't want that? Easy to identify, face and follow your truth...not always. But worth it? You get to decide for yourself. Your happiness and well-being hangs in the balance.

In the absence of identifying and resolving your natural feelings, the mind can invent further distortions or layers of defenses such as a sense of superiority. Superiority is a psychological defense for a feeling of inferiority (i.e., an inferiority fear is at the core of the superiority feeling). Superiority can lead to such distorted emotions and emotionally immature behaviors as controlling, bullying, hatred, discrimination and violence. Not only are others hurt by these distortions, so is the individual harboring them, even if they do not appear to be on the surface. They carry the burden of low self-worth in their core, and their happiness and well-being will be greatly negatively impacted by such low energy, unhealthy thoughts and feelings.

The following chart depicts the process and consequences of following your true or natural feelings from your heart's (i.e., soul's) wisdom versus getting stuck in the mind's distortions.

Follow your true feelings

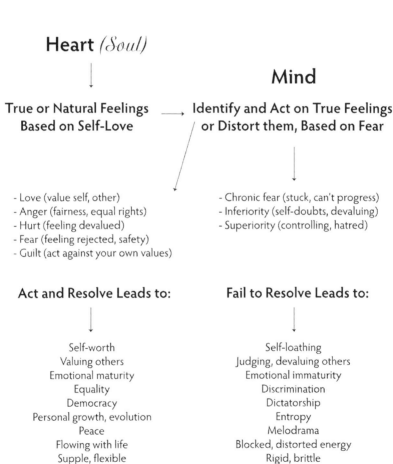

Heart *(Soul)*

Mind

True or Natural Feelings → Identify and Act on True Feelings
Based on Self-Love / or Distort them, Based on Fear

- Love (value self, other)
- Anger (fairness, equal rights)
- Hurt (feeling devalued)
- Fear (feeling rejected, safety)
- Guilt (act against your own values)

- Chronic fear (stuck, can't progress)
- Inferiority (self-doubts, devaluing)
- Superiority (controlling, hatred)

Act and Resolve Leads to:

Fail to Resolve Leads to:

Act and Resolve Leads to:	Fail to Resolve Leads to:
Self-worth	Self-loathing
Valuing others	Judging, devaluing others
Emotional maturity	Emotional immaturity
Equality	Discrimination
Democracy	Dictatorship
Personal growth, evolution	Entropy
Peace	Melodrama
Flowing with life	Blocked, distorted energy
Supple, flexible	Rigid, brittle
Health	Illness, pain
Happiness	Depression, bitterness
Love	Fear
Life expands	Life diminishes

Emotions are our driving force—causing us to act. We learn how to handle them in childhood in the context of our families. How were the five true or natural feelings handled in your childhood home? Where they identified and expressed directly and clearly? Or where they expressed indirectly (e.g., non-verbally) or not at all? What was modeled to you by your parents? Were you encouraged to voice all of your feelings or just a few of them? How do you express your true feelings or heart's wisdom now with your partner, with your children? How do you deal with their true feelings? Which of your five do you tend not to recognize or express?

The next time you notice you are having some feelings about an issue, take a few minutes to inquire more deeply into your heart's wisdom or sit down with a pen and paper and go over each one of the five. Ask yourself, are you angry i.e., does something feel unfair to you? Are you also hurting i.e., do you feel devalued or unloved by someone you care about? What do you care about (or love) pertaining to yourself in this situation? Is there someone else involved, and if so, what do you care about (or love) regarding them in this matter? Are you afraid to own any of your feelings or say them out loud? What do you fear if you do? Are you afraid you're unworthy? Do you fear being rejected? Are you afraid for your safety? Do you feel guilty about your own actions? Have you gone against your own values? More often than not, you will discover that a few, if not all five natural feelings are present in you regarding any given emotional issue.

Resolving conflicts or how to fight fair

In order to develop self-esteem and to improve the quality of your relationship—meaning establishing trust, equality and closeness with another individual—you will need to fight fair. The aim of a fair fight is to resolve *the feelings* of both parties equally as best as is possible because the fight is perpetuated by the failure to resolve the underlying feelings the issue has created, not the issue itself. (You can argue about the issue forever and never *think* the same way about it as your partner. But if you are able to resolve the underlying *feelings* equally, you can stop fighting, live with the different perspectives, and feel okay, even good, about it.) The focus of the fair fight is on *emotional* resolution as opposed to focusing on the rational or logical solution. When you resolve (ease or alleviate) the feelings of both parties equally, love grows — for the self and for the other.

The driving force of the resolution process is the feelings. In the context of the relationship, feelings are information about you and your partner. The first step is for you to go through the list of five true feelings and identify your own in connection with the given situation or issue you are wanting to resolve. That is, the first step is for *you* to inform yourself about *you*! Then, you inform your partner about you. You will need to identify and express your feelings clearly and directly, out loud. And then you will need to be informed about their five feelings which means listening. The challenge at this point is to put your own feelings on hold while you are listening and learning about the emotional experience of the other. Remember, your feelings are based on your perceptions about the issue or topic. They are a reflection of your own inner truth and guidance system (core values) and will also reflect the parenting you received and your life experiences. The combination or degree of the five feelings you experience will be unique to you and different from another's because we all have different "truths" and we all have had different experiences. In other words, your feelings *are right or true — for you.* The other's feelings *are right or true — for them.*

When you express your feelings directly to someone, you are saying — this is my emotional experience of the situation or issue.

(Note: A helpful exercise you can utilize until you get comfortable with this method is for each party to acknowledge out loud the feelings they have heard from the other. Remember, acknowledgement does not mean agreement. Simply state that you hear the other feels a given way. This helps to eliminate lecturing or yelling, which people often resort to if they fear that their feelings were not heard or will not count equally in the solution.) The solution is one which addresses or eases (resolves) your main feeling(s) while also addressing or easing the other party's main feeling(s), simultaneously. In other words, both party's *feelings* are of *equal value*.

Handling your feelings in a mature way, in other words taking responsibility for your feelings, means identifying them and expressing them in language that informs (not blames) and conveys them to the other. Taking responsibility means owning and resolving your own feelings; it does not mean that another person has *caused* your feelings. Also, others cannot read your mind, and you need the *experience* of identifying and speaking your own feelings. It is an essential part of developing your self-esteem. Identifying and informing another of your feelings does not mean blaming or criticizing. Identifying, expressing and acknowledging feelings in this manner are processes whereby you are relating to one another on the basis of trust. You trust your partner to listen, and to value you and your emotional experience and not to reject you for having your feelings. That is, you trust them to *empathize*, but *not to agree* with you. In other words, you are asking another to put themselves in your shoes, and to believe that you are honestly conveying what seems to you to be your true feelings as best as you can. And having received listening, empathy and trust from the other, you then offer the same to them as your equal. Following this process builds the trust between the two of you and you will feel closer.

Once both parties have clarity regarding their own feelings and those of the other, the intellect comes more into play to generate and negotiate solutions. Do not suggest a solution prior to both parties having had a chance to sort out and own their feelings out loud. That would be the proverbial "putting the cart before the horse" and will likely not provide a long-term resolution to the problem. You cannot arrive at a solution that is fair to how both parties feel unless both parties have said how they feel! Remember, the solution needs to resolve the feelings of both parties equally as best as possible. The final solution based on the feelings may involve a 50/50 compromise (which appeals to the logical mind) but it might not be. If you feel less strongly than your partner does, you will slide more their way on the issue and vice versa. However, you will both *feel* that the solution has addressed your emotions *as equals.* And as a result, not only does your own self-worth strengthen but you will feel a more intimate connection with your partner as a result of increased empathy, trust, negotiating as equals, and easing or resolving the feelings of both parties.

In the absence of equality-based communication processes, the opportunity to resolve the feelings and foster the self-worth of *both* individuals *is lost.* And, in the absence of both parties expressing themselves in this emotionally-based, equality-based fashion, one party will likely feel dictated to, or inferior. Or, one party may deny their feelings and acquiesce to please, rendering the other superior. Not only is self-esteem *not* fostered in these circumstances, inevitably, the problem will resurface and you will find yourself and the other party having the same disagreement over and over.

Mishandling, distorting and failing to resolve feelings

Mishandling your feelings means you fail to take responsibility for them. In the absence of taking responsibility for your feelings, you are unable to resolve them, and in the context of a relationship, you make the other party responsible for them. This leads to such emotionally immature patterns as blaming the other for how you feel, leaving the other to guess your feelings, controlling, withdrawing and alienating. In the face of these emotionally immature patterns, inadequacy or inferiority fears grow and self-esteem diminishes. Inferiority feelings can lead to crippling fear, animosity and aggression. At the core of such distorted emotions is low self-worth. Here are several ways feelings can be mishandled.

> **Failing to identify and speak one of your five true feelings:** This can be done unconsciously i.e., by autopilot, meaning that over time you have learned to deny and thereby avoid dealing with one of your essential feelings. You may have learned to cover one up with another. For example, you express how angry you are but do not realize yourself that you feel hurt and therefore fail to state how much the issue has left you feeling not cared about by your loved one (hurt). In this case, you have covered up your hurt with anger. Or, vice versa — you state your hurt but fail to acknowledge to yourself (and consequently to the other) how the situation feels unfair to you (anger). You have covered up your anger with hurt.

> You might also fail to own (acknowledge directly) one of your feelings consciously or knowingly because you are uncomfortable (fear) expressing it. For example, you may think that expressing hurt is weak, so you hide your hurt and express only your anger hoping you will be seen as stronger. It takes courage (i.e., self-love) to express your hurt, so it is just as strong to express hurt as anger — maybe even stronger — because you face your own vulnerability in the process.

➤ You might "hint" at the feeling (state it indirectly) or "suggest" to the other that you have some kind of feeling by acting it out (e.g., slamming a door or giving the silent treatment). This leaves the other to try to do your emotional work for you by guessing your feelings. It is a lost opportunity for the development of your self-worth and it is likely to lead to hurt and anger in the other. Instead of resolving the situation, this emotionally immature behavior will perpetuate it.

➤ **Criticizing the other:** You criticize the other for failing to read your mind, thereby failing to take responsibility for identifying and stating your own feelings. (E.g., "You should just know how I feel. Isn't it obvious to you?!") Or, you may be critical of the other for having their feelings. (E.g., "You're wrong for feeling that way. You have no right to feel that way.") Here you take a superior position. Your feelings are "right" and theirs are "wrong". You fail to acknowledge that your feelings and those of the other are of *equal value* – their feelings are *right for them*, yours are *right for you*.

➤ **Projecting your feelings onto the other:** This means that you see the feeling as belonging to the other person (i.e., you project it onto them) when really it belongs to you. If you are projecting, you have failed to acknowledge your own feeling. For example, you think your partner is angry about the situation, when it is *you* who is angry about it.

➤ **Blaming the other for your feelings:** This is another way you may fail to take responsibility for having your own feelings. (E.g., "You make me feel hurt or angry or guilty, etc.") Here, you see the other as *causing* your feelings and fail to take ownership of them. Remember, your feelings are *yours* — and stem from *your own* inner guidance and life experiences. Your feelings are based on your perceptions or how things seem to you. It is important to own your feelings. (E.g., "I felt angry and hurt when that happened. ")

➤ **Acquiescing to please:** This is an example of failing to have your voice — you do not state your feelings on an issue or in a given situation. Instead, you internalize your feelings and go along with the other's, thereby leaving yourself out of the resolution-making process. This is an example of emotional dependency, and a fear of being rejected is at its core. It is a lost opportunity for you to speak your truth and strengthen your self-worth.

➤ **Mishandling caring/love:** This means you have failed to express your natural feelings of caring or love to another whom you are close to. This happens when you allow your feeling of love for another to get buried entirely, or you show your love only indirectly (e.g., doing things for them, physical affection) and do not *also* state it directly. If your guard is up and you are too afraid of being rejected to express your love and instead say nothing, then you are mishandling both your love and your fear by not stating either feeling. (As stated, the *experience* of clearly and directly owning your feelings and stating them *out loud* is essential to the development of your self-worth.)

➤ You can also fail to love yourself. When you care enough about yourself to acknowledge and resolve your feelings, you feel *happy* about you and about your life. *Owning and resolving your feelings is central to self-worth and to your happiness.*

➤ **Mishandling anger:** An example of mishandling anger is when you feel wrong or bad (i.e., false guilt — see "Mishandling guilt" below) about feeling angry so you do not voice it. It is also mishandling anger when you withdraw when you are angry, or if you cry when you are angry and in either case do not come back as soon as you are able and state directly what feels unfair to you. (The latter is an example of covering up your anger with hurt, and the hurt is indirect [tears] unless you also state your hurt clearly with words.)

➤ Another way to mishandle anger is to keep repressing it until you blow up and scream, demean or physically aggress against the other. This is being aggressive (dictatorial) rather than assertive (democratic). Anger expressed in a critical, hurtful way, by screaming, swearing at or somehow demeaning the other results in your taking a position of superiority over the other. This distorted or pumped up anger is immature anger as you are trampling on the rights of the other individual (aggressive) as opposed to behaving as an equal (assertive). True anger is an expression of strength — it is based on your self-love (self-esteem).

➤ **Mishandling hurt:** You cry when you are hurt but you do not then put your hurt into words and state how you are feeling devalued or uncared about by your loved one. It may be quite natural for you to cry when you are experiencing hurt (or any of your five feelings for that matter). This is fine, unless you just cry and fail to state clearly when you are able to, which feeling you are "crying" i.e. having, and why. Just crying is an indirect expression of your feeling.

➤ **Mishandling fear:** You allow your fear to get pumped up and build to massive proportions by failing to identify it and speak it out loud which eases or resolves it (e.g., as in the case of a fear of being rejected by the other). Often, we use fear to cover up another feeling such as hurt or anger. For example, you are afraid to tell your partner that you are angry because you are afraid if you do, you'll have a fight (which means in its essence, you are afraid of being rejected by your partner). So, you internalize both your angry feeling and your fear about expressing your anger. This leads to covering up your anger with some other feeling, or withdrawing altogether. Do you recognize this pattern? Are you confused yet about your own feelings in this case? If you are, imagine how your partner feels about them?! The solution is to go forward, face your feelings, and state them anyway. (E.g., "I'm afraid to tell you I am angry, for fear we'll have a fight and you'll reject me — but I'm telling you this anyway!") As a result of owning your anger and facing your fear directly in this manner, you'll feel stronger and feel less frightened to state your feelings next time (i.e., your self-worth grows).

➤ **Mishandling guilt:** You feel "guilty" for having your feelings, but in reality you have not gone against your principles or values at all, which is *true* guilt. If you are mishandling guilt, you are using "so-called" guilt to cover up one of your natural feelings and need to explore and own which one of your true feelings underlies this "false" guilt. Often, we are afraid to express a particular feeling which we are uncomfortable with, or fear the other will be uncomfortable with it. Instead of acknowledging this feeling, we cover it up with fear and guilt and wind up feeling "guilty" for having feelings.

To summarize, acting on and resolving your true feelings is essential for strengthening self–esteem

The experiences of coming to an understanding of your own feelings, acquiring the courage to speak them out loud (speak your truth) and not reject yourself for having your feelings are vital to the development of your self-esteem. This is how you take responsibility for your feelings and prevent the mind from pumping up your feelings or distorting them thereby fueling fears of unworthiness and inferiority. And, when you participate in a democratic communication process which necessitates allowance of the other party's feelings equally, you feel better about *you*. *I.e., you help yourself to feel equal to the other* and your self-esteem is enhanced even more.

This democratic, emotionally-based method of communication is also how you help your child to develop their self-esteem. The central parental contribution towards the self-esteem development of their child depends on presenting a balance between unconditional love and realistic, consistent limits. In addition, as parents model identifying and expressing feelings, valuing their feelings and the feelings of others, resolving differences and achieving a balance between pleasing oneself and the other, they contribute life-time tools for enhancing self-esteem.

As the child matures, their concept of themselves or conscience is forming. Not a conscience in the sense of teaching or commandments, rather an ongoing process of formulating and refining their own values in the context of experiencing personal relationships with their parents and significant others. Facing new unknowns, especially fears, are central to this process of gaining knowledge, defining and acting on one's values, and "finding oneself" (which really means obtaining a strong sense of self-worth). Gender identity, an important part of our sense of self, is also evolving. It is influenced by parental attitudes and behaviors both towards the child and towards each other. Although their parent's contribution is central for the foundation of their self-worth, as the child matures and separates, his or her life-long experiences (e.g., relationships, education, health or illness, facing traumatic events, successful counseling, etc.) will all continue to influence their self-worth for their entire life.

Our awareness of our feelings is dictated by our level of emotional development which ranges on a continuum from emotional dependency (i.e., emotional immaturity) to emotional independence (i.e., emotional maturity). In the dependent extreme, the responsibility of how one feels is placed on the other person and they are blamed or seen as the cause for one's feelings, which are often expressed by outbursts and/or withdrawal. A person at the emotionally dependent end of the continuum may be greatly invested in controlling others, submitting to others, or a combination of both—hoping to hide their fear that they are "not as good as" or inferior. As stated, we all have inadequacy fears—we just differ in the degree of fear we have. One of the most common psychological defenses against owning inadequacy fears is a focus on over-achievement or perfectionism where one hopes they look good to others and it reinforces the illusion of self-esteem (it is in fact "other-esteem").

As we mature emotionally, we learn that our emotions are information about ourselves that is unknown to others, and that we have the responsibility to inform ourselves and others of our feelings. In revealing ourselves, we face our greatest fear—that being, we are not as good as the other (or inferior in some way e.g., we are bad, weak, stupid, ugly, etc.) which is the root of all other fears. In the process of being aware and expressing inadequacy or inferiority fears, the most significant product is the increase of self-worth. Also, we are then engaged in the process of becoming more emotionally independent. This is a long continuum in which the objective is to diminish inadequacy fears, enhance our self-esteem and discover close personal relationships. Regardless of where you are on this continuum today, regardless of your parental examples or your life experiences, you can learn and grow towards emotional independence and a feeling of self-worth or equality.

Equality

Charles Darwin was in the news in the year 2009 which marked the 150th anniversary of the publication of his 1859 manuscript, *On the Origin of Species*. His research, together with his subsequent work *The Descent of Man*, concluded that all species of life, all human races, all plant and animal species throughout all time are related through descent from a common ancestor, they are interrelated and interdependent, and that this evolution has occurred through the process of "natural selection". Such a radical theory of the time seemed to deny the tenants of his largely Christian society. Moreover, he lived at the time of 19th century slavery. His close family members were active as abolitionists. His research contradicted support for slavery that argued blacks and whites were a separate species and that whites were created as a superior race. All of Darwin's research supports the hypothesis that all races have identical roots and belong to the same human family. To Darwin, although races evolved differently, they were of equal value and should have equal rights. Evolution supported emancipation. Slavery was a sin. Since his death, his theories have been supported by genetics, biology, fossil record, comparative anatomy and the geographical distribution of the species of man. To date, no convincing evidence supports the notion that modern species are not descended from common ancestors. However, the many details of how this has occurred remain to be discovered.

The basis for liking oneself or self-esteem is also based on equality. Ideally, we have learned from our parents or guardians that our feelings are of value and may differ from others. We learn to balance pleasing others with pleasing ourselves. We learn to face our fears and assert ourselves to defend our values, and we understand and respect that others have the same rights. In any close relationship, our feelings regarding many situations will and should be different. (They will vary depending on our values and how we perceive the situation based on our parenting and life experience.) Although our feelings and those of our partner's will often differ, because we are equal, both sets of feelings will be equal to each other. If we learn to bridge the gap to resolve our differences by arriving at solutions aimed at alleviating the hurt, fear, guilt or anger of both partners equally, it will be possible to love ourselves and our partner independently and to feel closeness based on trust. Otherwise, we will find ways to control and/or submit actively or passively, we will have a more dependent relationship, our feelings will be guarded, there will be mistrust, and we will be distant from each other.

Darwin's society was based to a large extent on inequality which is the core idea that *On the Origin of Species* demolishes. The notion of "inferior" and "superior" formed the backbone of the society in which he lived and worked. Although in the present time this notion is greatly diminished, it is still a very potent force in our society and continues to spawn the notion of "right" and "wrong" (e.g., as evidenced in the issues of race—black versus white, gender—man versus woman, and sexuality—gay versus straight). Although lip service is given to the concept of equality in our society, in actual fact our evolution as a society will lag behind its full potential until equality is internalized at every level and reflected in a greater degree of emotional independence on an individual level.

In an emotionally mature, loving relationship, the foundation of this love is necessarily based on feeling equal to one's partner. To the degree that this is true, the quality of the relationship will vary directly — towards a closeness based on trust that is more reciprocal, more self-satisfying and more durable (as opposed to patterns of controlling, distancing and submissiveness, expressing mistrust and embodying the illusions of superior and inferior). This is true not only on a personal level with one's partner or in parenting, but also with one's affiliations e.g., towards their country, their religious beliefs, their philosophical and/or scientific beliefs, and globally, with their valuation of all life.

From time to time we wonder: Is it possible for me to enhance my self-esteem? Do I need counseling? Should I read a book or take a course, improve my appearance, or all of the above? Regardless of how helpful these courses of action may be, everything pales in comparison to the action of owning your own feelings out loud in a way that claims responsibility for them and never places the responsibility for them on anyone else (i.e., emotional independence), and which always includes the fact that your feelings are based on your values and perceptions which may be at odds with those of others. Nevertheless, your feelings are right or true for you, as their feelings are right for them. The rational (intellectual) approach to differences i.e., to argue "right" and "wrong", can never address changing the feelings but can only escalate the disagreement between you and the other party.

Every time you identify and express your specific fear and gradually alleviate and/or conquer it, you will feel encouraged, more confident and stronger. Every time you identify and express your anger, you are defending your values and your equal rights. As a result, you will feel stronger and worth fighting for. When you identify and express (mature) guilt, you are more likely to gradually change that part of you which you dislike, and again will feel stronger (and not appear to others as "perfect"). When you express your hurt (as different from anger) you realize that you are sometimes necessarily vulnerable and that hurt is an integral part of loving and is also a feeling worth airing in order to alleviate it in the future. And when you express caring or love (although in that moment you risk being hurt), you know you want and deserve closeness because you are lovable and with acceptance, your self-esteem will be reinforced.

All of this is a gradual process, a learning process towards personal growth. You need to experience this in the context of real life caring relationships as this is the primary and most potent arena to strengthen your self-esteem. In addition, other life experiences also contribute opportunities to add to your self-esteem development as you learn to face and express your feelings in a new, mature way—as you face, for example, a new job, marriage, illness, job loss, parenting, and other new adventures.

Yes, you can learn new communication techniques, read books, and attend lectures— all act as an assist. Yes, you can choose to get some help via counseling, especially if it seems that conflicting fears are presenting an impasse. The good news is that although your patterns of handling your feelings to date have been learned and reinforced out of habit, you can choose to change them and move to more emotionally mature methods which aim towards pleasing yourself and significant others, equally.

The best news of all is you have the power to be free! You are already equal. And you can gradually "know" this emotionally.

Chapter Six

REVITALIZE YOUR LIFE

*I*n navigating through daily life, we tend to think of ourselves primarily as a body or a mind and forget that we are so much more. The greater part of you is not in physical form. Who-you-really-are is consciousness which is Source energy, an aspect of which is currently focused in physical form. Because we forget that we are mind, body *and* spirit, our tendency is to pursue one aspect of ourselves at the expense of the others. You are not just bits and pieces, body parts and cells. You are matter permeated by mind. And on another higher (and lighter and faster) level, you are intelligent energy, permeated by consciousness — a spirit or soul. You are light, permeated by love. You are the *whole* of it and it takes a return to *wholeness* to feel happy and be healthy.

You are a creator currently focused in physical form in order to create and experience the physicality of life. You make choices all the time which affect all-that-you-are on different levels. But creation happens on *all* levels. Your body may want something, your mind and soul another. If, for example, you are thinking, feeling or behaving in ways that are unloving to yourself or others, or are making choices inconsistent with your own core values, then you are not honoring your tri-part self. Or, if you are devaluing your body by not treating it lovingly, you are again out of alignment with who-you-really-are which is *love*. In both cases, you are not acting as *one*. This means that the mind, body and spirit that you are will not be in harmony energetically which creates mixed results in terms of your physical life experience. Disharmony brings unhappiness, boredom, anxiety, depression, and/or disease.

Your soul will benefit and continue to expand as a result of all that you experience in this lifetime. But you don't want to wait till you're no longer in physical form to enjoy it and reap the benefits! *You* planned on creating a pleasurable physical life for yourself on Earth or you would not have chosen to be here. When your choices are in alignment with your well-being at all levels, the most amazing experiences will occur — you will manifest your *heart's* desires (but maybe not all of your *mind's* desires!), experience great joy and feel as though you have fallen in love with life!

If you are not feeling good about yourself or the life you are creating, the good news is *you* are in charge of creating your life. If you think your well-being and experience of happiness is dependent upon other people or having things that you cannot have, think again. Your mind has got you living under an illusion which is not serving you! Fear-based, egoic thinking has taken over. If your fears are telling you that you are not enough, or do not have enough, or that you cannot create a happy life for yourself, or you can only be happy when…then change your mind about that right now! *Remind your mind* that you are in charge of it; it is not in charge of you! The biggest way people give up their power is by believing they don't have any. You can take back your power anytime and make new choices which will change your life. Start today! Finish this chapter and implement change immediately. Pick the suggestions summarized in this chapter that appeal to your heart the most. Start with just one or two changes and build up to more over time. Breaking an old habit and creating a new one takes a good measure of focus and energy at first. Taking on too much which is new all at once is likely to result in your sticking with none of it.

It is never too late to make change. In fact, contrary to what your mind may try to convince you of, change is easy to make because change is what life is all about. You are always only one choice away from change! However, in order to manifest the sort of changes you are wanting, you need to be focused in harmonious alignment with *all* of you. That is, your mind, body and soul need to be on the same page. Also, a strong measure of patience and determination is needed along with self-loving thinking, feeling and behaving. It takes some time for the Law of Attraction to align the energies of the Universe to help you create your heart's delight. Start with asking for and focusing your attention on commodities which can be created relatively quickly by the energy that you are and the energy that is all around you. For example, set your intention on having more laughter or opportunities for fun to come into your life; ask to be moved by something beautiful or an act of kindness; ask to experience something inspiring, or to have more love in its many forms come into your life — and see how quickly it happens.

Putting it (and you!) all together, the following sections provide a summary of the insights and suggestions offered in this book. May they inspire you to make some new decisions which please you. The effect that a change in any one of these areas will bring is not limited to that one area. All-that-you-are will be impacted.

Mind makeover

A crucial ingredient to taking back your power and being able to focus the energy of your thoughts on creating what you want in your life is to make up your *own* mind — about *everything*. What do you believe in? Why are you here? What are your unique talents? What do you think is right for you? What are your core values? What kind of life experience do you wish to create? Your life experience will be shaped by the perspective you take, and perspective is subjective, not something which is "right" or "wrong". Make decisions according to your own values. But however you choose to view it, your perception of life will influence your experience of it. If your thoughts and ideas are not working for you, change them.

> *Every decision you make—every decision—is not a decision about what to do. It's a decision about Who You Are. When you see this, when you understand it, everything changes. You begin to see life in a new way. All events, occurrences, and situations turn into opportunities to do what you came here to do.*
>
> *Neale Donald Walsch (1943-), author*

Think outside the box. Practice asking, "What are the infinite possibilities that I can have…that I can achieve…that I can experience… that I can feel…" And, "In what way(s) do I have *right now* all that I am wishing for?" For example, if you want more money, see where you already have abundance in your life. If you want a home you like better, focus on what you like about your current accommodation. If you want to attract a loving partner into your life, focus on the love you already have in your life (even if it is the love for you, by you!) Find the way you already have *in essence* all, or an aspect of, what you are asking for, and then you will shift your vibration to a positive match for what you are wanting to attract more of—like attracts like.

Reevaluate your definition of "abundance" and then see how rich you are! If you put your attention on all that you have, you will always have enough. If you focus on what you don't have, you will never have enough.

Remember when the going gets tough, look at the situation from an eagle-eye perspective. Float up above it and see it from the Grand Scheme of Things. Look for the learning embedded in the situation. What pattern is repeating? What is pushing your buttons? What do you need to see? Find the light in the dark. Get the intended growth. Remember the old proverb, "When it is very dark, you can see the stars."

Look into the mirror of the other especially when someone else is catching your attention or pushing your buttons. See what you dislike about them and also what you admire. What are their strengths and weaknesses? See how *you* embody these same traits. This helps you to stop judging everyone and yourself so much. For whatever you see in the other has been/or still is an aspect of yourself as you journey through your life and evolve.

Be open and even eager about self-inquiry, building your self-esteem, and your journey of personal growth. What did events in childhood teach you about yourself? What are the old, conditioned beliefs you have about yourself or others? What is it time to release? What is it time to embrace? Who are you? You get to choose. What are your goals, dreams and values?

There is an equal and opposite energy in everything on this planet of duality and the pendulum of life swings in both directions. Expect change. Expect to experience both ends of the continuum. If you are on the "negative" end of the continuum, once you've looked for any learning or growth that can be gleamed from the situation (the "positive end"), do your best to let go of it and row your boat gently along with it (i.e., go to the middle) — for with less resistance from you it will pass more quickly, or at least your upset feelings about it will pass more quickly.

Life works to bring you back to the middle. Life is inclusive not exclusive. You can work with the flow of life by coming back to an attitude of allowing, of wholeness. That is, come back to the middle of the continuum by thinking, "Oh, this is interesting." Or "Well, that's life." Try to see the opposite side of a given situation even if you do not agree with it.

Try to go with the flow of negatives, or of change which is frightening you. Remember at the molecular level, you are mostly water — the most flexible substance of all! When you, like water, do not flow life becomes stagnant. Change, no matter how challenging, prevents life from becoming boring and facilitates your growth and expansion.

No sooner do we think we have assembled a comfortable life than we find a piece of ourselves that has no place to fit in.

Gail Sheehy (1937-), author

If we don't change, we don't grow. If we don't grow, we are not really living. Growth demands a temporary surrender of security.

Gail Sheehy (1937-), author

Remember to bring your attention back to the present moment as often as you can. Stay in the "power of now" which is the only moment you truly have to live.

Plan for the future and set goals, but try to remain flexible and not overly attached to them. Avoid being too rigid or structured as the energy that is *you* will have a difficult time flowing, becoming blocked or distorted instead. Remind your mind that you cannot control everything. Plus you cannot know the "why" and "how" about everything in your life — your mind *and* your soul are co-creating the circumstances you encounter.

Keep an eye on the mind! Watch out for excessive fear-based thinking. Fears narrow life and get in the way of achieving one's desires. Fears also tend to magnify with age, which narrows life further. When fears become too thick, life becomes stagnant or depressing. Do not let fears get the better of you. Fears bring entropy. Ask yourself, "What am I afraid of?" Answer honestly. After identifying it, the next step is to face your fear and resolve it as need be. Facing your fears brings growth and expansion.

Fear tells us that we are inadequate, helpless and separate. Love affirms we are great, powerful and connected. Which voice — head (fear-based) or heart (love-based) — do you choose to be your guide?

Put a stop to the habit of focusing on problems. What you focus on grows! There is so much more right with your life than wrong with it. Keep your focus on what you are wanting and take it off what you are not wanting.

Put a stop to the habit of criticizing yourself and others.

Honor your mind. Respect it for the marvel that it is and continue to expand it. The old adage "use it or lose it" applies to many things, including the mind.

Body makeover

Perhaps no where is the tendency to criticize something as frequent and destructive as is the case with the body. Stop criticizing it! Criticism of your body is insanity coming from the mind. Remind your mind about that one! Focus on what is right about your body and what you like about it. Like your life, there is so much more right with your body than wrong with it. Honor your body. It is your temple and your vehicle to get around in throughout your entire life. You need it. Respect it. It works so hard for you, continuously, often with little thanks. Thank it! It is the only thing in your life which is truly yours, fully devoted to you and working non-stop for you. Spend time appreciating it, caressing it, loving it! Treat your body well and it will treat you well.

Listen to your body. Do not ignore it. Do not tune it out. Tune *in* to it. Your body is wise. It is intelligent energy and the "container" of the spirit that you are. What is your body trying to tell you? Ask it what it needs. Ask it what it would like to eat today. Ask it what kind of movement it would like to engage in today. Listen to your intuition which comes through your body first, then to your mind. If you are not sure which option to take, try each option on for size—imagine one option at a time and see which one feels better to you in your gut or heart.

Feed the body well. Today, a great deal of what we call food is, quite frankly, crap and we eat far too much crap disguised as food.

Make a point to read the fine print on packaging, or better yet, buy less of it in packages. If you cannot pronounce an ingredient or do not recognize it, avoid eating it. Demand better from your grocery store. Request alternatives without chemicals and preservatives. Ask them to stock local preservative-free options whenever possible. Support local suppliers if it results in more organic options. Supply will start to mirror demand.

Your body is built for motion—it wants to move, so move it! Movement is vital to keeping your body healthy. Find a mode of movement that you like (or at least do not hate!) and can stick with, preferably more than one, and get going—walk, climb, dance, cartwheel, lift, bend, stretch, run, swim, paddle etc. As with the mind, the adage for physical health is the same—use it or lose it.

The body likes regularity and routine. It needs you to adopt healthy, regular habits for eating, sleeping and exercising. Routine is good.

Given that your body is on the planet of duality, it likes routine *and* craves change! Breaking routine can be good too! You are here to experience the physicality of life. Take your body on an adventure. Or, let your body take you on an adventure. Dive in to the buffet of life with your body. Collect more experiences.

If you are ill, you will need to listen to your body and your intuitions most carefully. Rearrange things in your life so that you are as loving to yourself as you can possibly be. Healing is a tri-part being endeavor and requires your body, mind and spirit to work as one. Healing involves not only intellectual awareness but also emotional awareness. Physical transformation comes with believing things in your mind (intellectually) *and* in your heart (emotionally). Face the challenge and the feelings of fear and victimization that the illness will inevitably arouse in you, head on. The issue is not so much the illness but the loss of power that the illness activates in you. Go on a quest to find the things you can do that help restore a sense of personal empowerment. Make decisions that bring strength and power to you and dwell on your strengths and successes, no matter how small. Gradually, your feeling of victimization will diminish and your sense of empowerment will increase. You will feel that you have taken charge of your illness rather than it has taken charge of you. Be patient with yourself and the new steps you are taking to feel better. If you have a chronic illness, you did not develop it overnight and will not find relief from the symptoms overnight. Healing may not be curing. Seldom is there a cure for chronic illness, but a measure of healing and some relief from symptoms is always possible.

Spirit Makeover

In truth, your spirit needs no makeover. It is perfect just the way it is. It is the mind which says…I am not enough…I would be worthy if…I am happy as long as…or I'll be happy when… Your spirit or soul knows you are enough, you are deserving, and you are equal just the way you are. Your soul is always a part of you, always guiding you, always loving you. Although the loving energy which is the soul is always there for us, we can do a good job pinching ourselves off from it. It is the mind which slips into fear-based thinking and pulls us away from the guidance of the soul and the flow of life. Your soul is fearless.

To decrease the impact mind-based fears play in our daily choices and actions, our spiritual life requires attention and cultivation. Remember, the mind does not know how to flow very well with life or for very long but your soul does. The fear-based, past-based mind distracts us from the higher qualities of the soul. The human spirit requires regular nurturing through a spiritual practice such as meditation, connecting with nature, or prayer. A spiritual makeover is about taking steps routinely to shift your focus from the intellectual and constant busyness and buzz of the mind, and connect with the quiet of your heart and the consciousness within. It is about loving yourself and connecting in love with the life all around you. Then you can hear the guidance of your soul. Then you can know the path you were meant to walk. Then you will experience the flow of life which is comforting, joyous and fulfilling.

Make time every day, even if it is only for a few minutes, for quiet communion with yourself or for meditation or prayer. Simply focus on your breath, or the images in front of you. Be, don't do. Connecting with the stillness (which is the Source within or your inner consciousness) will center and ground you. It is important for your well-being and vitality to take a break from the mental and emotional swings that life on a planet of polarity and constant contrasts brings. Connect with the love inside of you. Send your body love. Breathe it in. This will foster your connection with your spirit. And it will help restore the dynamic balance of energy within your tri-part being. If you feel a bounty of love, send it out to the world. Imagine it spreading to all life, and then coming back to you, uplifting you and the entire planet to new heights of love.

When you need to make a decision, especially if you are experiencing fear, anger or pain, get quiet and listen to your heart's wisdom so that it can guide you. Identify and honor your true feelings. Ask yourself, what course of action would love take? Listen to your intuition, your gut feel. Higher guidance is subtle but talks in many ways. Ask your inner guidance to reveal itself, be patient and pay attention.

Focus on and foster the development of the higher qualities of your soul. Clarify and evolve your higher or core values. Build your self-worth and your character. Cultivate honesty, courage, steadfast-ness, benevolence, kindness, love, generosity, wisdom, creativity, mindfulness, patience, humor and/or any qualities you consider to be of value.

Focus less on material things and more on relationships, starting with the one you have with yourself. See yourself as an equal. Work on loving yourself first. Then you have more love to give to others. Be the uplifting source of loving energy in your household, office, community, country.

Collect more experiences, fewer things.

Unplug from technology and plug into yourself and your relation-ships with others more often.

Try something artistic or creative.

Look for opportunities to include more laughter, fun and play in your life, all of which are qualities of your spirit.

 If you laugh at it, you can live with it.

Erma Bombeck (1927-1996), humorist

Be patient with yourself and others. Remind yourself that you are a "work in progress" and will be your entire life. Everyone is a "work in progress". You are not here in this life to be perfect. Just perfectly be.

Spend time in nature. Nature is Man. Man is Nature. You are truly one with all of life. Man has been entrusted with the safekeeping of the planet and all life forms. Respect all life as your equal. Devote some time and effort to uplift the animal and plant life in your area. Be good to your Mother — Earth, that is. Her body is your body.

Define for yourself what it means to have a *good life*. Remember that all other forms of life are endeavoring to have a good life, too.

Remember to see life from the perspective of the Grand Scheme of Things. You are so much more than what you see. You are a drop from the great ocean of all life, a spark from the Source of it all. Focus on your goals, your dreams. Reach for your highest potential. You are stronger than you know. You are the stuff of stars.

Remember, regardless of what you achieve, life is in the journey not the destination. *Now* is the only moment you really have to live.

You are not alone. Ask for help.

Revitalize Your Life Daily Check List

Aim to have a little of each item or experience in your life every day:

- ➢ Be in the moment, be fully present and drink it all in.
- ➢ Do something productive e.g., do your best in your work or home life, learn something new, or do something to work towards your personal goals.
- ➢ Move your body in a way that gets your heart rate up.
- ➢ Eat or drink something tasty and nutritious.
- ➢ Do something playful, fun or adventurous—it might be something creative or artistic.
- ➢ Enjoy a good belly laugh.
- ➢ Unplug from others and technology and spend some quiet time in communion with the Source within through solitude, meditation or prayer.
- ➢ Give and receive a loving touch (with another person, pet, or yourself).
- ➢ Thank your body and send it love.
- ➢ Send someone else or the whole of Mother Earth love (openly or silently).
- ➢ Take a few minutes to be in fresh air in the natural world.

Fall in love with life again

You are the creator of your life. On planet Earth, you are on the leading edge of thought which is the leading edge of creation. What you focus on grows. Against the backdrop of contrasts provided by life on this planet, your mind and soul are co-creating your physical life and all that you experience while in physical form. In so doing, all-that-you-are will expand and the All-That-Is will expand through you.

Your spirit's job is to remind your mind of what is in your highest good and why you are here which is to experience what your *heart* desires. This is the same as saying — you are here to experience what you value the most. Follow your heart's dreams and desires. Reach for them despite any of your mind's fears that you are not worthy or cannot attain them. When you focus on your heart's desires, the fears of your mind are quieted and you can hear the guidance of your soul which is helping you along the way. When you are reaching for what feels good and right to you, when you are navigating through life in alignment with your vision of yourself and your values, you will feel full of enthusiasm and excitement about your life. In that moment, you are in alignment with the energy of your soul, which is love. You are a vibrational match to the Source energy within you, the same power that creates planets. In that moment, your mind, body and soul are in one harmonious vibration of loving energy, your energy and juices will flow and you will feel that you are in love with all of life. When your whole being is in harmony and functioning as one, astonishing things can occur — life flows, synchronous things begin to happen, plans come together, dreams manifest into reality — in perfect order and in perfect time.

Your challenges in this lifetime are manyfold but they are necessary for your growth and you are up to them or you would not be here.

I'll say it again…you are stronger than you know. See beyond illusion and absorb as much of the Cosmic Truth that *feels* right to you. It is never too late to create a better life experience for yourself. *You are just one choice away from changing the experience of your life.* Get started today. You have never experienced "right now" before. *Now* brings a fresh supply of energy. *Now* is a new opportunity to focus on what your heart is wanting. Creation starts with each new thought. Revitalization of the body happens with each new breath which brings an explosion of oxygen to your lungs. Revitalization of the mind happens each time you push back your fears, move beyond old conditioning and focus on your desires. Revitalization of the spirit happens every time you hold love in your heart.

All in all, do you feel you are in love with life? If not, you can embark today on the process to recapture that feeling. I say "recapture" because as a child, you likely had many moments when you felt that way. Even when facing or living in difficult circumstances, children are likely to experience more moments of the wonder and joy of life than adults as they have not yet been exposed to and shaped by years of dampening influences from society and daily life pressures. You were born in love with life, and you can fall in love with life again. Think back to when you were a kid and recall the ways you explored and enjoyed the wonder of life: e.g., digging in the sand and playing in the waves at the beach, building a snowman or snow fort, lying on the ground and taking in the subtle shades of green and the smell and the feel of the cool carpet of grass underneath you, breaking a crust of ice over a puddle with your foot, listening to the boom of thunder and anticipating the lightening in the sky, doing summersaults or spinning yourself around until the world started to spin, studying insects in the yard or at a river's edge, jumping in a crispy pile of fall leaves, finding images in the clouds floating by above, trying to take in how many stars there are on a clear night, the taste of your favorite treat, feeling exhilarated flying down a hill on a bike with your feet off the pedals, the first time you touched the soft fur of an animal, or finger-painted, the experience of the first day of school, or your first kiss.

There is no end to the incredible experiences of life that you can have — new possibilities for experiences present themselves to you every day. So what steps can you take to fall in love with life again as an adult? How can you get your boat to go merrily down the stream? Hopefully, this book has given you many ideas. The essential steps are to bring your mind, body and soul together in harmony, and then *let go of the oars and go with the flow.* Are you presently lost at sea? Do you feel as though life's waves have tossed you overboard? Are you living like a buoy — anchored to the spot and being battered by the wind and the waves? The following is a summary of four fundamental steps to get you back in your boat and headed in a direction that will *Revitalize Your Life.*

Four steps to *Revitalize Your Life*

1. Get back in your boat

Start with deciding what you value most. Ask yourself several questions: What in life ignites your enthusiasm or passion? What holds the most meaning to you? What feels good to you? What warms your heart? What makes your heart sing?! What would you do *for free*? Look at what you spend your money on. Do you like adventure, nature, technology, travel, science, art? Do you like creating, solving problems, helping or healing others? Who do you like to spend your time with — children, adults, the elderly, the needy, the ill, certain personality types, animals? What are the elements of life that you like to work with most? Do you like to work with paint, fabric, clay, metal, paper, food, words, computers, plants, water?

 Let yourself be silently drawn by the stronger pull of what you really love.

Jalaluddin Rumi (1207-1273), poet, mystic

Ask yourself how you can serve the planet or humanity in a way that would energize you or light you up (or en-*lighten* you!) What makes you feel like you cannot wait to get out of bed in the morning? Unhappiness in life is a result of disconnection between the aspects of your tri-part being. If you are not hearing and following your heart's desires (soul), if you doubt your ability or worthiness to have what you want (mind), you cannot embrace life. Your experience of life will become automatic, robotic and problematic (body). If you do not know what you really like, if you are out of touch with what holds meaning in your heart, then spend some time in quiet contemplation with yourself and ask to know your heart's desires. When you follow your heart, more and more of your soul's wisdom (inspiration) unfolds.

2. Float your boat

When you have honed in on what you value most, i.e., you know "what floats your boat", you then have your "horizon line" or destination. Keep your mind and heart focused on your horizon line, your end goal, *no matter what*. Now your mind and heart are working together in harmonious vibration. Your body will experience a surge of healthy energy and you will start to feel connected to your own life again and to the Big Picture. Plus, the Small Picture of day-to-day life will start to get a lot more interesting to you. You will no longer be just going through the motions day in and day out. You will start to feel wonderfully *alive*. When mind, body and spirit are in alignment like this, the energy that is *you* magnifies exponentially. Your vibration will be high and your point of attraction will be strong.

It is important to remember that the process of creating the life you want is all about *action (i.e., energy)*. It is *not a passive process* whereby you simply "wait for the Universe to bring it" without generating your own strong energetic (vibratory) point of attraction for the Universe to operate on. Although it is possible that all you want will simply fall into your lap without your having expended much positive energy in that direction, it is highly unlikely. The Law of Attraction is all about *matching energy*. That is, it works to bring you a match, energetically speaking. The stronger *your* energy, the more powerful (i.e., stronger and or faster) the *response* via Law of Attraction will be.

If your energy is lackluster or inconsistent, the results (i.e., what you attract) will be lackluster or inconsistent. Your actions ignited by your heart—meaning the efforts you make, your focus, enthusiasm, determination, passion and other positive vibrations—create your point of attraction and draw more of that same energy to you. Energy may come to you in the form of inspiration or practical help including the people who are an energetic match to you and your project or goal. It is the pull of your heart (spirit) in unison with the actions of your mind and body which the Law of Attraction operates on. In other words, it is the powerful pull of your tri-part being in action and in harmonious dynamic (energetic) alignment that taps into the Source of all potentialities. This is how you, as a tri-part being, create. This is also why you need to pay attention to your mind, body and spirit and to keeping all aspects of *you* aligned with what you wish to create more of. Wow!

Keep on asking questions. (The quality of the answers you get depends upon the quality of the questions you ask!) Ask yourself how you have *the essence of* what you value already in your life so that you can put more of your focus (i.e., energy) there *now*. This builds upon the existing energy, or to put it another way, it waters the seeds already planted so that they can grow. You may have to dig deep or look at your life quite abstractly to find the ways you already have at *least some of* (or a "stepping stone" to) what you are wanting more of so that you can expand on it. In other words, try to find a way to link your day-to-day life to your heart's desires. Don't wait for all that you want to materialize. Focus on growing the aspects or essence of what you already have. It is easiest to build on your current foundation.

 I couldn't wait for success...so I went ahead without it.

Jonathan Winters (1925-), comedian, actor

If you cannot find an existing link, ask how you can begin to put an aspect of what you value into your daily life. Ask how you can *open or grow yourself* so that you can get more of what you dream about in your life. Ask how you can *expand* into the next greatest version of your grandest vision of yourself!

Ask how you can serve others by engaging in your heart's delight. If you need money to pursue your dreams, ask how you can get paid for spending your time doing what you love and providing something or a service to someone else. If you value it, someone else will value it too. (Note: serving others and getting paid for it, or being rewarded in some other way, is a win/win or fair exchange and the Universe favors fair exchange. Fair exchange is another way of saying that the energy of both sides of the equation is matched [Law of Attraction]. "You don't get something for nothing," is a well-known truism. So are, "You get back what you give out." And, "You have to give in order to get.") Ask with heartfelt intention. Ask with solemnity in solitude or in prayer. Perhaps you are familiar with the expression, "Ask for what you want, you just might get it." Float your questions "out to sea" — to your soul, to the Source within or the Source of it all — to the highest source of consciousness, wisdom, or love that you believe in. Regardless of to what (or whom) you believe you are asking, the important thing is *to ask.* This sets your intention which builds up the energy and begins to put the infinite mechanisms of the Universe in action to answer you.

3. Let go of the oars and pay attention

Letting go of the oars does not mean you do not "do the work" of pursuing your dreams (although when you follow your heart, it does not feel like work, or at least it does not feel like work you don't want to do). It means letting go of the details — the how, when, where, who and what ifs of it all. Although you take your hands off the oars (i.e., you try not to worry about or "steer through" all the small details), you still have your eye on the horizon line. That is, you know what the core or essence of what you value is. You know what *really* matters and you keep your focus and efforts fixed on that point. However, you do not know in the final analysis where *exactly* on the shoreline your boat will end up. You let things flow and float into place, rather than forcing them. You let the details more or less take care of themselves. (I.e., you don't sweat the small stuff.) You cannot yet know the exact picture or the way your dreams will manifest. Stay open, stay flexible, live in the question, "What are the infinite ways I can experience more of…" Or, "What are the infinite ways this could work out or come together?" Let go of the specifics or the exact outcome you may be envisioning. Let go, maintain positive energy (e.g., your focus, determination and enthusiasm) and allow the power of your mind and heart/soul to guide you and bring you (via the Law of Attraction) the necessary ingredients (which may include people) to allow the creation of your desires.

Pay attention, for the answers will likely show up in subtle ways, signs or messages from others. Remember, it is the mind that screams and shouts at you, or verbally "hits you over (or rather inside) the head". "Energetic messages" i.e., guidance from your consciousness or spirit, while powerful and consistent, are gentle and oftentimes subtle. Guidance may come from an inspired thought, a gut feeling, a dream, the next article you happen to read or TV show or movie you happen to watch, or it may be delivered by the next person to come along who happens to mention to you a book, a course, a service, or offers to help you themselves.

Inevitably, your mind will start to generate worries. It will start to shout at you that you cannot possibly achieve such things. Your fear-based ego will inevitably tell you that you are lacking something vital or are undeserving in some way. Worries will cause your boat to drift away from the horizon and cast you out to sea. Bring your mind and heart back into alignment by refocusing on what you want and doing everything you can to stop your doubts. Your job is to stay focused, be patient, and pay attention (and enjoy yourself along the way, which keeps your energy positive). Now you are navigating through your life awake or fully conscious so you will not miss the opportunities which will begin to unfold. Your true feelings, intuitions, insights, messengers (e.g., in the form of other people suggesting options, opportunities, introductions, books, ideas etc. to you), coincidences, dreams, signs, etc. will provide you with guidance. Be sure to listen, watch, learn, experience and flow with it all.

4. Enjoy the ride

Although this sounds easy, it is arguably the hardest part.

The only measure of success is the amount of joy we are feeling.

Esther Hicks, author

It is wise to try to do something in alignment or in close approximation with your heart's desires or core values on a regular basis. This way you will be laying the foundation now for what you want more of in the future, and the energy of what you focus on will grow. Nevertheless, in the final analysis, you have no way of knowing if or when, despite your best efforts, opportunities to make the changes you desire will present themselves. (You cannot know all the intentions the consciousness which is *you* has in this lifetime of yours.) So, although you have in mind ideas regarding what you wish to create more of in life, the bottom line is you need to focus on enjoying the life you've got i.e., "enjoy the skin you're in". Life is not about waiting around to have your "best moments". Avoid the trap of falling into, "I'll be happy when..." Not only will your energy become negative or blocked, and you will block the flow of the positive energy you want more of, you will begin to feel disappointed or depressed about life.

Keep your focus on the present, on being mindful of the now. Focus on what brings you a feeling of love, joy, appreciation and gratitude. This is the energy that allows creation to flow. Finally, do not forget about the health of your body. Your joy ride will come to a screeching halt in this lifetime if your body gives out on you!

This is how you bring your best to life and bring life's best to you.

These steps will bring your mind, body and spirit into one harmonious flow of beautiful, omnipotent energy. You will feel revitalized. Your light will shine. You will enjoy the ride of life you are on at the moment and you will be in the process of creating the next greatest version of yourself that your grandest vision can imagine! Wow! You are always a beautiful, incredible work-in-progress.

Every day tune in, turn on, wake up, be present, stay alert, take it all in, focus on what feels good, wait for the moment to unfold and reveal itself and then don't miss it. Decide today to recapture your zest for the wonder of life through new eyes, the eyes of your heart, and fall in love with life again!

I wish you a good life.

ACKNOWLEDGEMENTS

I wish to thank Michaela Sirbu — my Soul Sister in this journey to learn, grow and experience a good life along the way and to help others achieve the same — for her encouragement to write this book and for her vision and dedication to the creation of our platform to uplift others, www.LivingMost.com.

I am very happy and proud to include the wise and heart-felt contributions to *REVITALIZE Your Life: A Mind-Body-Spirit Makeover* regarding self-esteem and democratic communication by my mother, Lynn McKenna and stepfather Bernie McKenna.

To Warren, Lynn, Bernie, and Michaela, I am so grateful for your support and continued faith in me.

I am deeply indebted to the incredible works of the many authors that I have read regarding metaphysics and spirituality. Their books have had a significant impact on my thinking and the information and perspective that I offer to others in my psychology practice. The inspiring content from so many books has gone into the melting pot of my mind over the years, commingled with my own mind and heart wisdom and reemerged as my words in this book. And although I can no longer remember which particular inspiring bits came from where, there are several authors whose wisdom stands out and I wish to acknowledge their contribution, not only to my own effort, but to the global cause to uplift all of life on Earth: Dr. Deepak Chopra, Neale Donald Walsch, Ekhart Tolle, Ester + Jerry Hicks and Louise Hay.

Made in the USA
Charleston, SC
03 October 2011